Convivial Communiverse

Convivial Communiverse

POEMS

LUCIE CHOU

atmosphere press

for all denizens of the Planthropocene, vegetal, animal, and all things in between

for my family, who give me the great art of living

And living to tell

Cento Songlines

1

These green beings have made this planet livable and
breathable for animals like us. Lapping up sunlight,
inhaling carbon dioxide, drinking in water and
releasing oxygen, plants literally make worlds. They
not only hold the earth down and the sky up, they sing
in nearly-audible ultrasonic frequencies as they
transpire, moving massive volumes of water from deep
in the ground high up into the atmosphere.
—Natasha Myers, "Photosynthetic Mattering:
Rooting into the Planthropocene"

In the name of the bee,
And of the butterfly,
And of the breeze,
Amen!
—Emily Dickinson

Daisy

Her golden eye rimmed with rosy-silver lashes
Is a tiny hub of vital heat
Beaming genially to warm early waking bees'
Chill, chafing hands and feet.

Dandelion

Dandelion, dandelion,
Sunny dews wake you blooming;
Warm and gold, manifold,
Bees find you and start tumbling.

Gloriole golden you gaze and glow,
Gaze and glow delightful.
Dandelion, dandelion,
Don't close your eyes till nightfall.

The purple physiognomy of aquilegia
Peers from profound petrous crack
Like a witch concealed from persecution,
Pulchritudinous and dark!

Wisteria Waterfalls

A vibrant violet, a prismatic purple
When pouring in live flow;
Spread out tranquil in the underpool,
A pale, cool, restful blue.

Iris

The messenger-maid of myriad selves
Is afield.
On a mysterious mission from
The plant-world.

She comes summoned by Arethusa's
Sprouting scream
From the garden hose hampering free flow
Of her stream.

The rampant saliva shattered to the sun
Makes fluid flesh
Flimsy, fuming, with whom iris's plasmas
Intermesh.

The fountain nymph's espressos of pain,
Light's elan,
And full spectra of prismatic generations
Are begun!

Fecundated by their poignant eros'
Ecstasies,
Earth repeats her name myriad times—
Irises!

From the marriage of water and light
In the air
Iris comes elucidated, her colours
Spread out clear!

From amalgamation of water and light
And the air
Iris comes efflorescent, her phytosouls
Everywhere!

Puce, violet, fuschia, saffron, lily, lilac, gold,
Bird's eye blue,
All the furbelows flounces ribbons beards—
All of you!

Tulip Cosmology

This barren, balefully bland spell
Has all zeal from itself banned;
Banished all basics of living well
From its browbeaten land.

But such disheartening tyranny
A tulip's ruddy fist cannot quell.
The valves wax rosy then fiery
Of this revolutionary rebel.

Then bleak times turn to blue bliss
Which burns her heart to braver pulse
Bursting out to a crimson chalice
Holding a newborn holy universe.

At its nadir a black detonated star
Rays out dazzling golden fleece;
From there rises a triffid pillar,
A beacon for beneficent bees.

In six cases rests this world's future
Carried by stamina on high.
Stardust falls to fecundate nature
Time to come will fructify.

Platanus

Socrates, alleging "trees and the countryside would not teach me"
Spoke eloquently of the psyche in the shade of a plane tree.

Sacred to the convection of words between philosophical minds,
It's a tall, patulous Platanus orientalis that the pilgrim finds.

Aristotle and Plato's canopied schools heard its susurrus.
A kin colossus stood in the garden of Lucius Licinius Crassus.

Millions of times it spreads wide the span of its five-pronged hand
Plain as platos, its appellation in Hellas, the ancient sages' land.

Plenteous in the eastern hemisphere as the west, in arid as wet,
Palms pullulate to gown the pulchritudinous silhouette

Against, on exquisite days, an empyrean as azure as the Aegean.
What gay sagacity, what gorgeous courage of the golden plane!

~~~~~~

Emblem

In our lovers' favorite garden grows
A dark-leaved evergreen tree
With florets the hue of ripe honey
Deliciously dating the bee;
In Mediterranean mythology
It is a divinifugal maid
A sympathetic magician
Transmutes to a verdant shade.
Stilled into green, growing eternity
By a magician's timely aid,
Her virgin soul by vegetal change
Inviolable is made.
Of the brisk girls and brave boys embracing
In the bower of that laurel bay
How many know that against violent lust
She won Nature's indemnity?
~~~~~~

Hymn to Sylvan Shamans

Let me
Into your
Communal cloister…

Shower me
With your
Vivified shimmers…

Calm me
With your
Balmy breaths…

Guard me
With your
Heavenward arms…

Fold me
Into your
Photosynthesized fibres…

Teach me
Your tunes
Of cellular xylophones…

Coddle me
In your
Cauldrons of chlorophyll…

O, in summertime,
Spread your shade over me,

Come autumn,
Shed your sere shit on me.

Treeconomy

Autumn is the austere reaper
The besom is an idle sweeper
A tree is its own housekeeper
Who recycles its waste.

Pussies and bunnies need cleaning
Parrots and wrens want preening
A tree would fain forgo pruning
To topiary's taste.

~~~~~~

Eyedom Is I-dom

En route from my dorm to our daily bustle
there is a boulevard of eyebark poplars.
Each stately, stretches its elephantine folds
of pale grey skin to open rhomboid opēs
to stare. Those rhombuses have round ink-gall-hued pupils.
Some lids are barely lifted apart. Some vertical and wild.
Some seem perfect but purblind. Others, gashed, with
black effluvia, gaze so poignantly that
the gazed's eyes bleed alike. The upper lids of some
are arched to gothic proportions, as if inner forces
push them to aspire to the estate of spire.
Some are emulsions of hemorrhage. Some are walled.
Eyes expand where the partition between self
and world is all but disparted: at forks, crotches, groins.
The most attenuated tegument. Some exert at one great
single opening onto the external. Others fragment
consciousness into a half dozen of fenestrae
that huddle tight like the just-wakened cells
in a morula or gastrula. Every predawn, every noon,
every gelid evening I perambulate this row
thousands of minute but nontrivial tectonic shifts
appear to have been effected in their eyedom.
I think of the ego. My "ego" thinks of I.
Or is eyedom an I-dom? Yes. That is why
with each eyebark tree and momently
the ophthalmognomy is a refreshed mystery.
~~~~~~

Broadleaf Bluster

Vigorous winds whinny though myriad palmate leaves,
Irradiating whimsical brilliance, limberly bending
Rebounding, as if instantaneously growing, decaying,
Inconstant and ingenious,
Dauntless and relentless,
Individual and indefinitely divisible,
Surrendering to and subverting
Susurrous swerving supple celerious strength of air
Iterating with their ecstatic elasticity
Mutable synergy of radical luxuriance
Argent melisma of verdant rhythmia

Ventilating an elemental language
Innovative beyond any inbuilt idiom,
Reeling raving ranging rhapsodic trees
Give glistering, inter-grating meaning to gusts, green groves
Alogon, atelos, aperiton, athanatos

Petulant Petunia

Petunia:1815–25; <New Latin <obsolete French petun tobacco
—dictionary.com
It's [the tobacco] a powerful plant. The power gets angry when misused.
—Joy Harjo

(Sniff a feral petunia. Nares become mistified by its ranc[1] mistery.)
Is a scent-ient being.
It has ordained an oblique stem
To pitch across the parapet's
Tessellated tiles
A sinuous succulent virescent tubule
Napped with a translucent fuzz
Leafily tremulous it says
A nifty bit of nicotine
Is a virtuosic thing it intimates
In delicious silence
Scent-ience lies not in nocuously
Binding your delinquent osmic desire
To my divinely indefatigably desirous odor
But in bearing four pale violet hearts
In painting pliant goblets gorgeously pink
In dabbing the lucent magenta with pollen
Scent-ient of syringa, lemon and jasmine
Vanilla, absinthe and cream of mint
Insouciant scintilla and scarified lawn
In smelling precisely like an impudent petunia
Whose impetus pelts puissant philters
Filtering a phytoplexity of perfumes
Into all physical apertures

It means Petunia am not a poison
Petunia am not a panacea
Petunia am not a pulchritudinous furnishing
It grows Petunia am more
It phanein *Petunia amo*
It languages Petunia am aperiton, beyond anything Human
preaches

---

[1] rank 2(12th ed. COED): OE ranc 'proud, rebellious, sturdy', also 'fully grown',
of Gmc origin.

Or interprets
It swirls proud pink
It overpowers all respectable
Speculations
It petuniates
Plenarily petulant passion
Pflantastically fungible funk

Matriarch of Gilt

for the much-maligned Canadian Goldenrod

When the ground is gold with
the meek dead of ginkgoes
she goes afield with her guild
carrying their own gilt.
A fuzzy, feathery, filamentous gold
flowering fecundly along
their granular bodies' filigree towers
of grace and power.
She knows their art
yearns to be wrought
from branching
and burrowing (all the time
carrying their composite
gilt flowers on their
gorgeous bods)
interspecific marrying
and maleless carrying
traveling by tortuous
attentively tenacious
tentacularly torturous
trammels
athwart tracts and
through thoroughfares.

The insignia of her guild
is this Golden Rod.
This solidly built, gilt
Solidago shooting growth spurts
yellowing many a sod.

Her Yellowweed is a weedy brood.
Their creed is brave truth.
Just a soft, slight brue of blood
then a flamy yell
a yellow bellow,
a billowing flood.
Dread nought in going
to every field
growing strong and profound

even if this bids to wound.
Go Solidagoes!
Bathmism!
Chrysobatos!
Go louder!
Glow prouder!
You are your god
Golden Rod!
Gobble sky and soil's booze!
Spoils free-for-all, abuse!
Bear and broider bruises!
Cleave, chastise and root-coil
all shoddy clod!
You are your god
Golden Rod!

He is a cowardly crook
whose glib globe-guarding
gostronomical gobbledygook
groks but his own Golconda
(which must never be
gibed, galled, gashed
by her guild's flowing
glowing gilt rota)
and glozes over his garrote
of her guild's gilt skin and flesh
by orgulously
calling their gallant gaiety
oikological guilt.

Guilt?
What is guilt?
It was when his thoughtless goldthirst
grabbed her and hers away
by the root to gild
their alien assharts
histie and gross.
It wasn't when the rage
(or was it joyride)
of their gilt efflorescences
just rose
got errant, and spilt.

Guilt?
Heed not that hateful epithet.
That flagitious lilt.
Its force finds no hilt.
Gaia is gravid with gilt.
Striated like samite.
A web of gilt volition guy-wires,
refulgently, it all.
What power holds it whole?
Her godlike gestalt
gone feral
and ferociously fond
of branding and bonding beings
with their bowers of flowerful gilt.

Monofoil
Kingdonia uniflora

I am a weed.
Hailing to no name.
Grown from stray seed.
I have no fame.

Only likenesses:
Aquilegia,
Wood anemones,
Daucus carota.

They are like me
When leafy only.
But never more
Come their famed flowers.

Florid prestige
Pressures, constrains.
Like genteel siege
Laid to their brains.

I'm free to dawdle
Byzantinely
With thread and needle
And filigree

To sew my foliage
Lobe by slim lobe,
Scallop the selvage
Nimbly as a nib.

So I'll be gruff,
Slight, drab, and poor,
But wondrous enough
Not to bore.

And it's futile
For flower guides
To state a style
My life abides.

Florazure Is Only Ours to Give Away
—*This lyric is a gift.*

We are morning's precocious glories
Gleaming dewily in pre-auroral hours
When the horizon's first blush is hoary
Flaurora's miraculous azure is only ours

Our complexions are aglow with blue
From twirling open to jay-hued day
Sparkling sapphire zephyrs endue
Us with fleeting azure only to give away

In anthocyan harrowed hearts rejoice
Salved by our cerulean service of sedative
Azure aureoles will flower no invoice
Only enjoin the graced gratuitously to give

Vernal Bulbs

daffodils
crocuses
hyacinths
trilliums
tulips
choinodoxas
every March
oozes
lithe blithe
luminous juices
from the liquefying
linctus of primavera's
avid albescent skies
to incandesce
your bulged bulbs
your flammable hearts
crammed with accrued
translucent lard
of sweet rage
in wintry coverage
you kindle kaleidoscopic
flickering flames
of pale gold
of seafog grey
of twilit purple
of lacustrine blue
of bleeding crimson
of intense white
cariad
cordial
heart arsonists
bulbous radicals
your plotting
roots plot
all year
beneath
this sylvan plot
only to light up
only once

your courageous outrageous
colourful fragrant
conflagration
to consecrate
your loved vernal wood
then strew
embers of hearts' mayhems
testimonial emblems
and go again
undercover
to recover
to remember
your radicle act
your emotion
an anthera
anaract
a fiery-go-aground
to resurrect

To the Dragon on a Trellis
White Woodsweet
Rosa banksiae

You stand
Sinuous
Sinewy
Strenuous

Bark pared
Flesh bared
Twisted cables
Dark red

Dried blood
Rough veins
Strong thrawn
Pillar of pain

Is this a prop
A whippletree
A pergola
A pillory

A garden
A forest
You spit fire
You howl flowers

Your corpus
A cord of gore
Your spew flames
White plumes

Partygoer
by *Pieris*

I return to the meadow's ball
A fertile mess, a free for all

From sugars made from a thousand suns
Clovers bake us buttery buns

From tipsy goblets of the bloomy bindweed
I imbibe an inebriation of mead

I see a bee shove her velvety glove
Down the violet vulva of her love

And know this is no genteel party
That I'll get all my tentacles dirty

So walk to wallflower after wallflower
Sharing with each life's crowning hour

And swing dance, and sashay, insouciantly,
Sprinkled with wind-spores' unsolicited joy

~~~~~~

Dragonfly, I Will Praise You

Where there is an eye
Of water, there are you
Buoyed between ethereal blue
And the deeper rippling blue

Your self is a speck of sapphire
Sailing swerveless through the air
Like a halcyon pulsating star
Outblazing day's brightest fire

Your fashion of flight? A cross
Borne crystalline on the sunbright
Deck of your back, weightless
As sublimated ice
~~~~~~

Group Portraits in Miniature
Salvia paludosum

From the low-impact walkway
zigzagging over riverine
terraced slopes
marsh–mist blue

Convolvulus

Were you all once naked
virgin white and petite
like these petiolate snowflakes?

Did tall-tufted grasses
tip their brushes
in Aurora's pollen-cocktails
and pinken your goblets?

Were the azure cups
once plucked by Leonardo to funnel
copper into a bear's poisoned grimace
then rehung on the trellis?

Burgundy-ruddied infundibula
did creation imbrue you as intinction?
Your vinous vacuity holds no but
is a sanguineous sacrament

To Grass—

Dart-sparging brushes
you embraced me in
your bristly bosom
and baptized me as
your bur-bearing angel

Let Me Drink at Thy Fount

A poet eats a plant
ethically—

she perches within plashing
distance of an imposing
grass's oatmilk fountain

and summons her
nutritive numen
to upwell to her skin

Persimmon

Come fall
let me repair to you
to pick up scraps
of your sloughed
saffron parchment

On these
I'll write poetry

A pulchritude
it pullulates
and putrefies

Etude for the Aerobat

I love how your name is also a name of the Muses,
Pierides. Pieris, Pieris, it is felicitous
That you, large white, ample-skirted butterfly,
Are namesakes with a shrub whose budding leaves
Blush like Aurora's astonishing youthful passion.
You are both Pieris. You both make art on Earth.
Your splendid panels are quicker than fingers
Skittering across the keyboard declaiming
Liszt's Sospiro. Your winged paths have wilder,
More whimsical and swirling and swerving
Somersaults than the pianist's digits, which march
Up, or down, in two directions only, while
Your improvised musical score is all over space
Capering carefree of staves of steel rails
And blithe about the bars of palisades.
Your strength and dexterity exceed the athletes
Racing on the brick-red track above which you walk
In crooked curves, seeming not to care a dime
For speed, yet flickering faster than those
Bent on winning the trophy of velocity.
They practice running, then sharply turning,
Turning, running in the opposite direction,
Suddenly sprinting, braking, turning back,
While you swing insouciantly higher and higher,
Gentle flicks and strokes of ivory sleeves,
A sheer shimmer of motion and music.
But you, too, have served apprenticeship
In wormhood, when you carved your choreographs
On the chlorophyll pages of cabbage leaves
Before easing into the theatre of ether
Batting wings, agile as banter.

Com-menting with Chlorophytum comosum in Chthulucene

in homage to Donna J. Haraway

will you play SF with me, green plant of luxuriant locks?
(beautiful hair appurtenant to no head;
your hair *becomes* your hands *become* your headless mind[s])
you are verdant and hirsute, holding forth
strong, spidery, full-arched branches, whose extremities
are both hair-hands and that with which they entrust
what is held out to. I see in this palpy outreach
of yours, spider plant fairy, a sagacious flourishing
of hope, hospitality, history, of holding your hairy lives
hostage to happenstantial love, of always
holding open all those helping hands to Earth,
of bravely bracketing all those young plantlets
of tufted ribbony leaves and fleshy aerial roots
to fabulate life's green hairy stringy routes.
Chlorophytum comosum, Green Plant of Ample Hair,
will you create SF with me? where SF stands for
string figures, species friendship, synnoiac flourishing;
Hairy Spider Fairy of the Green Plants, if you will,
Trailing from pots on my windowsill,
cut me one handful of your locks to carry,
with both my humble human hands,
with lively loving curious care,
cat's-cradle-wise, not to keep but to relay,
but to lay out to land, to save by setting free,
setting in humus, fostering with hot compost,
to sow the future for spider fairy fecundity
that synthesizes photons for sympoietic felicity.

Circumnutating in the Chthulucene
for Cayratia japonica

When you bind a vine
With the bine of a vine
Will the vine be twined
By the bine of the vine?

Men name Me
a muscular   or
a murderous   vine

Oh but Magica is my middle name
Magical Me   I am
an extremely   excellently
intelligent   vine

I twine wild wiry wily bines
all round strong foreign plants
Oh I'm much too witty
to make of Me a warp
        and Them a weft
or Me a weft
        and Them a warp
(I say Yes to Me   and No to You
my macabre dance   is not for two)
I always weave
a much more wayward   woof

My growth
        throws
                out death throes

                I garrote
                I throttle
I can be a formidable foe

a wielder of mighty mojo

But my ravaging spirals
have sober demurrals

to slay my own
thrawn   wroughten   wrythen
egos
however
multitudinous
                              sinuous
       tortuous
               tortious
                    sinuous
               flexuous
                                        anfractuous
they're never
too arduous
to recognize
(remind you
I have a brawny beautiful mind)

You inquire
How do you tell
a target of banditry
this green
is so knotted clotted woven
       woxen wood
       good god!
Well it's
elementary
for elaborate
Magical Me

(But you've no
neurology you say)

But I've a defter desmology

Because I have so many interconnected selves
all of which indefatigably circumnutate

My tendrilselves   stemselves   shootselves
       sway
               in circles
       infinitesimally
               small

                    slow
                  steady
                scanning
                  stout
                stable
              whole
         wondrously
      sentient
             they
               skywrite
                ley
              lines
          that
            feel
          welfare
             or ill-will

That's the way
            they
try out how
          to tender
                      disparately
                tender
mercies
depending on whether
it's Me or Them
they meet
(and much more
they meet   intricately
                              holistically
                horripilationally
they mete
out such multiplicitous everythings)
                      winch   windrows
                    wrench   woody bones
                  clinch   with stubborns
                  cinch   traceried mullions and transoms
                  twitch   at the touch of ache
                flinch   from harming their own
              blench   from mitey gossamer
            pinch   a matey hook
          punch   an evil beak

I have rhizaselves too
        wedded wendingly and tight
     in a wood wide web
          a commons
               all connected
          like a convoluted wealthful
            healthful
     internet
   routing their lives
        by drawing sensitive circles

up   down
all through their
                labyrinthine
                    shelves

                              below
                              subfusc
                              ground

                              so touching
                              so moving
                              this sounding out
                              of all surrounding
                              by soft somersaults
                              makes   rootselves
                              roundly ready
                              securely sound

they live
beyond   rivet   rift
or cleft
they are under
impossible to sunder
violence may
bend or prescind
but my mind
(in so many folds
so-many-souled
so-multi-selved)
never
not connected
bound or resplined
none can rend

In that
resides
all my swingeing wonder
subtle magic
svelte strength

I am a creature of the
chthulucene
surly
unruly
burly
braided
married
burgeoning
ramifying
lo
my
mazy
matted
meandering
mystifying
marcescent
matrices
a mess
a mesmerizing
myriad frame
lo
my
raven
swart
rotund
racemes
a miraculous
mephistophelean
million

Flora's Party

Will you tilt down the verdant goblets poised in your budding
    hands,
My dear liriodendron, tulip tree?
Vernal woodlands flow with more colorful cups than my eyes can
    drink.
Golden and vermilion paisley swirls and fractal lacy rims adorn the
    gay vessels.
When I place my curled fingers around the underside of a rosy
    tulip,
I fondle the blushing silky cheek of a blossoming damsel.
A tiny hill of deep red daisies—delicate heads of maroon teddy
    bears with bright beady yellow eyes.
They stand slight and low, in little ball dresses of sweetest
    ultramarine, puff sleeves clustering round their slender arms,
    blue-blooded grape hyacinths.
Your complexions are myriad—brick red, pale purple, butter
    brown, greyish blue, etc. etc.—but one and the same are your
    radiant azure eyes, ox-eye daisies!
Canola blossoms, dazzling daubs of cadmium yellow bobbing on
    their lanky shins, remind me of Luna Lovegood in her sunny
    dress robe at Bill and Fleur's wedding, insouciantly brushing
    buzzing snargles aside.
Second-month blossoms kirtle up their limp pinkish purple skirts,
    their greenstick legs showing through their pleated plackets.
Pisum sativa, blood-dots spotting the pinnate feathers of grass.
I see the twinkling wings of butterflies painted by the palette of
    the citrus family—lemon yellow, tangerine orange and lime
    green.
I see the pastel blue wings of day moths frequenting clovers.
I see two butterflies waltzing higher and higher, farther and farther
    into the empyrean.
Rosemary, you are blue as Virgin Mary's exquisite robe of lapis
    lazuli.
Wisteria, pensive, drooping, cascading, in both hue and odour
    such a delight.
Borage, hairy fairy, you have no perfume but the purest peerless
    passionate sapphire eyes.
Lonicera, twine your ribbons and tie your bows on the verandah.

Viburnum! you are the kingdom of buzzing bumblebees!
    odorantissima, macrocephalum, tinus.
Quince, portmanteau of Queen and prince, quiet eldest daughter
    of Pomona, are you here?
Cerasus japonica! Pyrus pyrifolia! Peaches, apples, cherries, plums
    and globes and juneberries, on steep slopes pliantly weaving
    branches of proud clouds, gaudy and lush, an orchard white,
    pink and red, yet mysterious and intimate like Goldengrove.
I hug the pale grey trunks of poplars.
I clamber along the rocky dwelling of mountainous plants.
I have pulsing growth under my soles.
I sniff the infinitely subtle scents of a thousand unique souls.
Yellow magnolia smells like molten butter, and burgundy red ones
    like wine.
Small floribunda daffodils and white Pom-poms are distinct in
    their inebriating sachets.
I kneel down and there is this tuft of wildflowers reaching out
    white-sleeved forearms with flaring sky-blue ruffs and semi-
    pellucid tassels.
I am surprised by a breath of sweet piercing aroma and turn to the
    tally: xanthoceras sorbifolia, or shinyleaf yellowhorn, with
    snowy cornucopias of crêpe flowers poking diversely from a
    groovy bole.
Weeping elm, your new leaves are hued like duckling-down.
I see trees from the spurge family and the borage family—newly
    discovered kins.
I remember the euphorbia tree has deep-veined carmine leaves on
    long straight strong wands, like a flamboyant covey of
    strutting flamingos.
I remember a top-heavy redbud tree whose fat flowering flesh has
    not one streak of purple sanguinity but is all smirchless white,
    almost seraphically bright ,effervescent with hungry droning
    and eager buzz.
It seems the vestal ones are favorites of bees.
I remember a cultivar of tulip called "world's favorite" and reflect
    on how all are the world's favorites that come out in leaf and
    bloom in such a sublime spring.
I recall an unnamed shrub whose soft yellow pentamerous flowers
    my first impulse it is to approach and inhale, oh to be
    answered by its serendipitous heavenly scent!

When the buff lawn is flowing gratefully with the wheaten gold of
    late afternoon sun, I lay my eyes on the gently poppling lake
    young with purple foliage of aqueous plants.
It is so lively and placid, all at the same time.
The plants!

2

The red dawn now is rearranging the earth
Thought by thought
Beauty by beauty
—Joy Harjo, "Morning Song"

...journeys outward that are also about finding
home, finding a voice, finding a way, finding a
place.
—Peter Quigley, *Housing the
Environmental Imagination*

Nature offers us a wonderful place in which to
dwell. One and unique, it is also always
changing and becoming, according to the
seasons and the geographical place.
—Luce Irigaray, *Through Vegetal Being*

A walk is doubly an act of witness
Through a tunnel of green light
Filtered through films of foliage
Or across grassy open site

To both the body of the outward world
And the world inside the soul
Constantly being reconstituted
As season and space unroll.

In the explicit terrain and firmament
Blossoms and berries come ripe,
Bees, birds and butterflies busily
Drop by and depart with a swipe.

And the unformed elements of the mind
March apart to grounds and skies.
When Goldengrove is inward grown
The heart is Paradise.

December 25th, 2021

1. I peregrinate like a potentate

   I peregrinate my sovereign land at predawn hours, before light comes trooping in. It is darkling and soaking. I put my senses to test. I sniff damp rimy grass buckled and softened by cold sluice. A keen gale nips my nape.

2. It is niveous

   It is niveous when I walk out into the boulevard carpeted with platanus duff. Streetlamps stage an autonomous tenebrae. Each head of brightness bears an aura, is a temenos, in which whimsical flecks whisk about. The glorioles go dim. A grey lackadaisical light rises. The skies are low-clouded, canescent, niveous.

3. Abiding in nature's gentle violence

   Abiding in nature's gentle violence, I am at a loss. I query, Should I embrace the weather's terrible beauty, or should I avert face and body, a refugee? Do I stand in the lifting gloom to anticipate the coming, do I express fear and reverence by seeking shelter within centrally heated walls?

4. The offertorium

   The offertorium is the mute scattering of snowflakes into puddles riddled with willow leaves. Eucharist and Mitzvah. A brunch of bouchée for my feline friend. I break the cake. It has a filling of strawberry ice-cream. When I lay the crumbs down before her meowing muzzle, it brims with whispering, wispy warmth. I am grateful to witness her shy grace of wrecking the nuggets of nourishment.

5. Plants live in snow

   Plants live in snow, spangled, glistering. Chimonanthus wears a chrysophyllous gown embroidered with sharp, aromatic, ametrine satiny wax-garlands pollinated by white evanescent crystalline pollen. Feathery pines refine their lightweight green by a superposed calcium redrawing. Emerald shamrock meadows erect trilobial ears, alert above the fresh-fallen snow. Out of season, heroic, violet syringa, sapphire veronica bloom. A gestalt of amulets blessed against chimatlon.

6. A pallid sun hunts for warmth

A pallid sun hunts for warmth by raising its flaccid strength above ironblack whitedusted twigtips, nebulizing falling flakes to a tender drizzle. He who aches for caring heat paradoxically gives it.

7. Near winter solstice, late afternoon

Near winter solstice, late afternoon quickly turns to evening like hungry quernstones hastily grinding corn. Dark. Humans lining up chatter their chill teeth like a busy mill. Friction between light and shadow generates miraculous ice-flower. Flour. So flurries of snow fly heavy against romantic chiaroscuro.

Snaweder

After the Beginning of Spring, It Dawns Snowing

When a volcano in Tonga erupted, the tephra ejected from the incandescent caldera consolidated into a gigantic solar barrier that incurred observable change in global climatological patterns. Temperatures went significantly lower and distribution of levels of precipitation was shifted. Inland China witnessed ,generally, a colder and more humid January in 2022 than in an average year. This impact persisted well into early February.

Brightening, whitening,
Snow does not wake into wide day
But delays a while in albescent darkness.
Whitening, nightening,
Air strokes snowflakes falling in families,
Huddling, hugging, holding together by frozen glue.
Nightening, lightening,
White-pinnacled pines and privets spacewalk
Laden with hoary glitter. Stubbly lands levitate.
Lightening, quietening,
Silence descends over the icing sugar.
A baking pan lying in wait in a vast oven.
Quietening, heightening,
Blackbirds compose their black oval bodies
Into a musical score on the sheet of white field.
Heightening, tightening,
Somnolent somas shudder at cold currents
Coming through shutters of open casements.
Tightening, frightening,
Come full daylight, a constantly strengthened contrast
Between evanescent white and evergreen viridian.
Freighting, unfreighting,
Heaven heavies and unheavies leaves.
Snow moils, amasses, melts, sublimates.

White Magic

Winter is the witching time of the year
Before Psyche's slumbering sororities
Awaken to find each other comelier
Transformed by Favonius's soft fragrant breeze.

The white witch limns the world's myriad skins
And their microterrains with frost and snow,
Plum trees' fine twigs, grass blades' long lithe shins,
Winter jasmine's shags with snags of yellow,

Cycads with long tongues lolling out, ice-tied,
Sinuous branches bared to braced sinews,
Frozen conglobulations of blood that bide
In sere rosebushes to burst their old bruise,

Snow's charisma of contrast and clarity
Stokes souls in hiding to hilarity.

Its magic's very brittleness and brevity
Charm heavy hearts to brief levity.

Into the nipping shrewd air we come
In ludic mood, casting away mild grief.
The light indoors can be gloomy and glum.
Out here, a gift lifts life into relief.

It's fleeting indeed, and ineffable
How it by its sheer simple stainlessness,
Transforms our staid minds with some transient spell
Into something like itself, briefly gorgeous.

So long as icicled trees and gemmed grass
Sojourn in the park's makeshift fairyland,
We'll frisk and fingerpaint on fronds' verglas
And mould mansions out of melting sand.

Windy Firs in Streetlight

1
Birdnotes and snowfurs
Stroll chill chiaroscuro
Few, faint, beautiful

2
As fuscous lucifers
Live these firs
With flittering twitters
Of blackbirds
And flocculent
Flying white winterfurs
Conspiring with the afflatus
Afire in their suspiring hair

Spring Bloom

When I came back to school beset by isolation and apprehension, I noticed a plum tree with multitudes of twigs plump with pink foam.

When I left in the joy of holidays, it was all wintry gloom.

Now, called to the new term's reckoning, I found spring abloom.

I had never felt the poignant complexities of emotion a gently blushing cloud could carry before.

In the ensuing days I wiped petulant tears of separation, back-grounded twinging fears of failure, and buckled down to con books in the library, where slashes of platinum gold spattered onto the strips of floor between shelves through slatted windows.

I walked out at lunchtime, when the neonate infanta of spring beamed her baby smile on earth with the strongest warmth.

My exams rolled along, day by day.

Parallel lines drew themselves through the ramose bodies of spring-blooming trees and strang them with fatter and flashier buds.

The beads, white, pale pink and dark rose, burst into ebullient beauty and subtle sachet; swarms of blues and bees suck at their taffeta breasts, sluing and swarming.

The mountain peaches lit the little lights along their slender parabolic branches, each one a star radiating five short rays of pastel pink, and the trees are vernal maids of honour standing placidly at the wedding of the air-god and the earth-goddess, cascades of blushful happiness laughing from their lush hair.

The exams drew to an end with the end of the week; on Sunday afternoon I went on a spring expedition with a girl whose heart was my unknown but natural kindred. She enjoyed walking, poetry, the seasons, and the implicit music of nature.

She was Hilaeira, the goddess of brightness.

She loved wintersweets and plum trees. We gazed reverently at their proud and expectant bloom.

The pale green plums came into their prime; the colour was cool, a sun-honeyed mint green, but the massive groves' merged canopies gave the impression of warm snow, snow hot with vital heat and dripping with the sweat of St. Hildegard's greening green.

We sniffed their softly whispered scent-melodies.

It was slightly grassy, earthy, evoking a prickly but pleasant hunger.

For all souls, spring is a time for nutrition and connubiality.

My companion and I sat on a round flat rock by the pond, our lanky rumps crowded like the small purple buds just beginning to bulge on the trees rocking their reflections in the quiet ripples.

We walked back to school as the clouds lying down to rest on the horizon were touched with twilight's rutilant blaze and the bright laughter of spring blossoms shake blithely in the shadowy evening's shivering breezes.

Vernalagnia

These refulgent days birds go routering-bout
And the first whites, greys, and blues come out
Fluttering and hovering.
Day in, night out, the valentining
Is never ceasing.
Blackbirds alight on the lawn with beaks red
As if lipsticked, feathers sleek and lithe
As sable tuxedos of the gentle-bred,
Their streamlined bodies slimmed of winter fat,
Their warbling unblenchingly blithe.
A magpie tilts her tonsured head
To tipple liquor from a leaky sprinkler.
The finches forage frolicsomely.
They look like bickering chocolate brownies.
Sparrows raise racket and raucous strife
As if the feuillemortes of the deceased year
Had come back to life.
All the avian infatuated flurries
Of fickle husbands and flighty wives!
And there's this gaudy gewgaw of a tiny god!
Scarlet crown, ebony eyepatches and startling white cheeks,
Matching black cravat above beige belly with croceate streaks,
A flowing bluish cape slinky as a halcyon sea
Tapering to the perking tail's indigo bay,
They jink and jitter jubilantly,
O hear their impatient jerks of harmony!
Butterflies jaunt trippantly through the air
Trawling for nectars,
Mellifluous lodestars,
Veering in swerving vectors.
Bees are strumming, thrumming,
Ahum, afuzz, abuzz, bumbling
With their burring bodies of sun-goldened ermine fur!
They drone through infinite realms of flowers.

These realms are ruled by flower power.
Every flower-soul famished through winter
Comes reborn to tryst with its lover.
The souls of azure veronica are deep and large

While the pallid ice-blue forget-me-nots
Are fond of more tinily treasured thoughts.
Borage looks through milky blue glasses
That cannot veil its lush cyan lashes.
Dandelions' souls are worn all over their leonine faces
And all their faces are luteous teeth
Shining in mouths agog for truant kisses.
Wild strawberries strip yellow cinquefoils
Petal by petal to search their lovers' secret souls:
Loyal, disloyal, loyal, disloyal, loyal!
O! He is leal!
The fairest virgins, the most intense,
Believe in amorous albescence.
A long, thin, pentamerous star is the chickweed's avatar.
The little cressoul sucks its four milky baby's fingers.
Souls of corydalis lift their arrays of slender pink hearts
High above shy tufts of intricate leaves.
They appear sheepishly happy and alert.
Up from verdurous rosettes of serrated hearts,
Purple blood is pumped into atria and ventricles
Of the labyrinthine lined corollas of violets,
And they palpitate, "Violet! Violet!"
As if their lovers are listening for that epithet.
These are the variegated spirits of wildflowers
Waiting for gaiety on the ground floor.

Some desire grows out of gaunt ground;
Some other bursts from bare boughs.
Pomona's bonny ebullient blossoms.

The maiden bosoms
Of early-blooming plums
Are embroidered with erythraean pom-poms.

The pastel mountain peaches
Preen their pink fleeces
To please the flirting breezes.

Short, stout, and shrubby,
On knuckles gnarled and knobby,
Duplex peaches wear blobs of ruby.

Crabapple, cherry and apricot,
Each flower's heart ineffably sweet:
Love's sacrosanct sugary treat.

Apricot, cherry and crabapple,
Canopies of crowded corollas dapple
Heaven and earth with white, pink and purple.

Crabapple, apricot and cherry
Flash in flurry after fragrant flurry:
Perfervid to fuck and make merry!

Butterflies and bees, flowers and fowls
Spring's powers ravish and arouse.
All are tasting the rapture of triumphant tryst.
Tryst is the place to wait in trust.
Every scintilla of the world's voluptuous body
Knows Primavera's lavish love
As a lichamly, luscious, ludic lust.

La Primavera

You are golden as a fresh lemon or bright cat's eyes.
Cascades of yellow jasmine are your hair.
You wear mezereon perfume on your plushy breasts.

You are azure as mazarin or prelapsarian air.
Your lawn-soft body can open myriad bird's eyes
To beam unblinking back at the cerulean skies.

You are pink as a bridesmaid's delicate doll dress.
Such ample folds to span the spectrum of shades:
From purplish magenta to pale pellucid rose.

You are white as ivory or an apple's fresh-cut flesh.
Your cream-sweet tongues singe through shells of fur,
Shed fuzzy embers, and cachinnate in candescent fire.

You are green as how love can light Scarlett's eyes.
In a thousand gestures you open your leafy fists
To fling out Chloris's wedding confetti with fanfare.

You are boisterous as a bijou bird with cinnabar mitre,
Black eyepatches and cravat, white cheeks and blue cape,
A perse tail perking from sides of soft saffron blur.

Rain Balm

Rain in spring has a whiff of grief in joy
And a jot of joy in grief. Pinkish white
Clouds of cherry blossoms glisten bright
On wet black boughs, shed scented tears, and pray.

Purple-leaved plum trees bring forth profuse bloom
Before summer's purple bronze foils outshine
The perfumed nebulae of ianthine.
Then efflorescence fizzes out like foam.

When rain falls to drench sun-parched ground, the smell
Of soil is grateful. When rocks give thank-yous
To water given by air, it's petrichor

That rises to mingle with the faint and frail
Fragrance of fallen, frittered flower tissues
That float on pools in the frondescent floor.

Religious Rites

Rain in spring is rich as sacred oil:
The Chinese do have a point.
The earth's the mother, sun the midwife,
And a drizzle there to anoint.

Bright birth of foliage and brown death
Of overblown early blossom
Are unified by pluvial benediction:
Slowly smirred clear chrism.

Fresh maple and fuscous-freckled magnolia
Both effulge with extreme unction
To commend one to magic unfurling life
And comfort the other's extinction.

Flower Showers

A romance so sumptuous
A favor so sacrosanct
To stand
In this snowing shade
Feeling soft   scented   onto my face
Dying love   saying grace

In Memoriam

The memory of spring
Is written in water
By the washy, clammy
Cadavers of flowers
Clinging
To damp pavior

A cloudless dawn in spring is a maiden
Unravished, uncoy, cool;
She has pale, raw, blemishless skin;
Her honesty is almost cruel.

Her large lacustrine blue gaze
Is energetic and erect;
Her streaming strawberry blonde hair
Is untied, untangled, undecked.

She slowly but steadily tends to her toilet:
A dress of apple green organdie,
Plain noiseless shoes, no stockings,
And a gay garland for holiday.

Not for such a free innocent spirit
Unpoisoned by experience
Is propriety's elaborate exhibition
Or modesty's affected pretense.

She exchanges ebullient gossip
With songbirds' brazen coterie;
The content is randy, raucous, rude—
But the cadence such melody!

Spring Storm

Willows feel love's ardor suddenly go cold
As its passion was violent its betrayal is bold
They forgo their meek demeanour and debonair
And wring their hands and rive their hair
And fling each mutilated body part
Wide apart to broadcast the outraged heart
Winged seeds from domes of plane trees
Range like down shed from cloudy eyries
As if goaded by the gales, eagles' golden chicks
Were keen to change feathers to try flying tricks
And the night over, the next morning is grey
Calm and overcast, blank of a tear or ray

I wander across a meadow of big-lobed clovers
Bobbing albescent burly spheres of flowers;
Alfalfa flutters bee-baiting yellow beads
That are the bright studs on the velvety meads.
At noon the shadows are solid and deep,
The sun's stare intense, trenchant and steep.
As day draws on heaven's light grows grey
With menacing clouds blotting blue away.
Winds whirl scents and sediments around;
Severed branches drunkenly run aground.
Dusk cooks dinner with hands damp and cool;
Green doughs are kneaded with flying drool.
Night kisses earth a good -night with wild eyes;
Lightning and thunder are its lullabies.
I tread across the petite prairie again:
Lamplit leaves glister with crystal rain.

~~~~~~

A noon in April is a full-blown damsel
By her gaiety made a goddess.
The favour of her cerulean smile
Fills all creation with bliss.

She has a bold blue beamy brow
Above an ardent bloomy face.
Her dimples hold fountains of plenty,
Her lips protrude to kiss you peace.

Having outgrown girlish garlands
She dons a shady broad-brimmed hat
Dappling bluebell cheeks with dancing steps
Of leaf-strained woodland light.

She's herself carefree with matters of dress;
But flowers, her fond sartorials,
Spray the most fabulous dyes over her frock
Flourishing with their furbelows and frills.

Her sublime yet spontaneous grace leads
All of nature's peoples in her train
To ride romping through gardens and roads
To parliament in the plaza of town.
~~~~~~

Spring is already abdicating,
Trashing her trinkets as Queen;
Outgrowing her gay gossamer gown
In the convent of cooler green.

She tears the garments that no longer fit
To colourful, corrugated tatters
From which the sun's strong, steady squeeze
Wrings ethereal, torrid attars.

A dynast of darker, denser shades
Brushes together these balms
To bathe and bless the beginning of his reign
Over the restlessly vital realms.

Summery Summary

Smell of softening rubber and pitch
And varnished wooden fence
The firmament's conflagrant blue
Converged by heat's swelling lens

Green is made greener, red redder
By the sun's white light and blind
His wheel rolls across our atmosphere
A daily great incandescent grind

Roses, honeysuckles, star jasmines,
Dogwood saucers, tulipwood cups
Line the day's sybaritic smorgasbord
Where at sunset a zephyr sups

Five Summer Scenes

1
Blackbird with cherry
(Ruby bead
Red bleb
Russet bauble)
In its beak
Black beauty
Bringing awing
Booty berry

2
Mosaic quadrats of blossoming white clover
Above which quivering shadow-bees hover

3

Birds Revenant

Swallows
        seldom seen
to skim
        the sublunary
                sphere

swing   swirl
low enough
to swipe
                    the sunny sward
to gall
                the glistening grass

What are their
    agile
            adumbrations
                omens
            for?

Volant umbrifers
you of the swift shadows
you know
                before
we know
that   there is
a something   to know—

4
just when
aestival ardor
has said
          OBLIVIATE!
to orchards
of March
amnesiac anthema
of apples
apricots
almonds

in May
when heat
has wafted
temperate
blooms
away

you pour forth
pure albescence
with full force

your aroma
nameless
intense

rosaceous
eidolons
redolence

5

Aubade

morning
   courtyard

morning
   parterre

morning
   fishpond

morning

scarlet palates
of oxalis
suggestively
opening
to probing
tongue
of sun

white lips
of waterlilies
letting a little
light flow out
floating
lotus
lanthorns

ooooooo
ooooooo
oral orifice
at the omphalos
of morning

oporostomata
open to
oriental orgies
& osculate
auroral
oriflamme

Earth in Adolescence

My body is raging.
Heated with red hectic humours
My hormones are horrifying.

My green folds of skin once interleaved
With cool, clean, nonchalant petals
Are inflamed with pink pimples
And purple pustules

Full of pulsing ebullient
Pulpy pus. Sparrows and blackbirds
Pick at my spots of hot pain
Suck out the translucent juices
The ruby eddies of my exquisite blood.

My body is hot and sweet.
The poking, prickling pique
Of beaks teasing
My itchy patches, my aches
Almost feels like a treat.

Levin Trees

Each
lives
lit from
firmament
for a brief
bright   branching   blink
rooting   through
voluptuous   aestival   heat
with   swift   splitting   cells
of   sapphirine   snow
shot   through
with   silvery   slivery   ice
then   blooming
into
a blinding   blue Bo

and breaks

its gelid

dendrites

down   to a descending   drenching   deluge

of

pur   ple   plu   vial

pop   pling   drop   lets

of   dark   ling

di   op   si   de

Cloud Lauds

Praise vicissitudes in whimsical skies.
Praise looming nephological shapes.
Praise bright clouds and livid.
Vapors condensed and rare. Praise skiey bodies.
Praise souls. Praise water-inky shades.
Lightish cerulean openings. Praise slight sultriness.
Praise light that augurs rain. Praise
Moist mossy smells that do not mell.
Praise the ratio of plumbeous to white.
Praise the ratio of white to sapphire. High, hunkering,
Hoary, hyaline, hyacinth. Praise the widening
Beam. This expanding Mediterranean.
Startling shadow-trees erumpent on concrete.
All things becomingly accepting sun's gleam.
Praise sombre intervals. Praise
Bluey waters shutting eyes. Black puffy eyes
On the brink of weeping death.
Some flutter open. Some close for rest.
Praise myriad warm capable eyes waking this palimpsest.

Prothalamium

Being alive this morning makes all desiderata decease.
I just wish to marry the vegetal world.
As I jog under the pearl-grey blooms hanging the cerulean ceiling
 of her bridal chamber,
My knees go not weak, but wantonly vigorous.
The vegetal world, breaking her rainy fast on ebullient light,
Calls me to caper higher and higher, stride wider and wider,
To be worthy of her wild delight.
I scamper among her long slim shafts of sage green shadows, and
 cry, silently,
"Will you marry me?"
She answers, "If you rejoice when I revel,
If your mind grows a little greener,
Your spirit a little freer, your verve a little vaster,
Your senses a little more in communion
With my osmanthus odours and wisteria colours,
My mossy comfiness and overripe fruitiness
My hale late prime, my craving for a last spree of light,
If you open your breath unto mine,
When you exercise, when I photosynthesise,
When all my verdant surfaces wake and rise,
Then come to me, then come to me, then come to me."
Her minty scent and chrysanthemum spectrums blaze and bedazzle
 me.
Her chinaberry canopies and bamboo bushes refresh and nourish
 me.
Her blooming golden rod trees and dripping firs shower me in
 confetti.
Oh why not, why not woo and win one such as thee!
But I impugn my own nubility.
I am grey and dull like aged plaster.
I am sterile and skinny like a stony skelf.
Perhaps I have no lovelace to tie the knots.
But I need not remain so.
At least, when I humbly lay my penury before the vegetal world,
She reassures and comforts me so.
"Let us marry and take joy
And invite other worlds to join our jubilee.
Marriage will enrich our mutual energy.

Make love to me! Make love to me!"
Then into the slightly acid smell of autumnal gingkoes
Into the fine etched silhouettes of backlit pines
Into the ponderously fructified persimmons
I run and run and run
With rapturous reverence and filly-like frolic
And give all my being to the Genetrix's generosity.

Dendromopoetics

I embark on a jogging jaunt into the woods. For all the Saturnian
shadows swagging low above the sparsely populated Saturday
skyline, the showers that softly soaked the past night have ceased.
Throughout the concrete roads' atlases of shallows and holms,
heel-flattened ghosts of sere leaves.
Dun, soot-whelked, skelloid
Serrated hearts for poplars
Toothed fans for gingkoes

> Celebrate falling
> As you praise our increasing
> Time on both depends

The elements recompose themselves every moment I look, while
I myself am in motion. When I run, the sedate, static font of
reality shivers into a flourishing cursive. The canescent firmament,
a gargantuan hyperborean animal, plays with its plumbeous whiffs.
Cicadas whicker. Blackbirds warble. When I turn a corner I am
reading a new line of a musical score. What with the Holy Ghost
of our living world becoming particularly hot and humid in her
aestival love, bark of pagoda trees, chinaberries and elder poplars is
splashed several feet high with emerald, muscoid nap. In and out
of the deep-water light greened by interlaced canopies of maple,
dogwood, purple plum and bamboo I jog, my immediate
inhalations and exhalations jiggling a few inches from my silently
whinnying lips.
Darling trees, I breathe
In your breathing-out's ample
Momently-made boon
I strive hard to breathe
Your lifeful mouthfuls

> You who are other
> We must mutually mother
> We swill your prana
> We spill your manna
> Air, hear hosanna

Azaleas are ablaze with crimson and roseate corollas. The rich
pink, nodular, whimsically warped carps of magnolias like cute

minuscule dragons nestle among yet unyellowing leaves. In the
cool armpits of osmanthus, silvery green sparks for September's
sweet scent are already simmering, sizzling. Golden flames flower
in tree crowns. When rain has drowned a small proportion, the
strewn embers smolders days more, fulvous.
I combust inside
My capering uncalm soul
My fiery gas green
With what our mutual
Open lungs converse

We burn on our skins
Air birds bugs swerving seasons
Blaze sets them blooming
Growing and running
We respire we sing

August 30th, 2021

A flavescent leaf
Swings, somersaults, arabesques
In morning traffic

September Psychosphere

Summer in dotage
Sprinkles soft moist sorrow on
Her sun-wrinkled smile

Two Haikus

★

Air repastinates
The nephosphere. A peep of
Blue bedrock laid bare.

★

Not scarlet but mauve
Runners puff out wee folded
Chartaceous balloons

Autumnal Compunction

1
Not belonging to one's place is a crime.

So is living outside of one's time.

When will I dwell at ease among my dwelling's alien lineaments?

When I have received its seasonal sacraments.

When the place has given me to experience its experience of time.

2
Haply I will partake of the plane-tree festivities.

Let the rutilant strata of strewn palps be my matrices.

I will have a golden foliage burial. Hours later I will have a golden
 foliage rebirth.

Slow combustion of moldering duff will be my hearth.

I will jovially join the plane-trees' death jamboree festivities.

3
That rubescent maple (the most patulously plenteous I have seen)

Salutes me everywhen I depart for home or get back in.

When its art of anthocyan has schooled me how the blushy can be
 brashly bold

And how the hibernal heats up in hue to outface cold,

I might brave strange fears same as the tried and seen.

4
Those moping willows will weep a swiping valediction.

Paulownias will whittle themselves to wrythen skeletons.

The question about these lavish actions of last passions is: in what
    weather?

Weather is the aegis that shades me and trees together.

Will reappear as a souvenir of valediction.

5
My compunction needs trees to complete; they are fierce.

All my existentiality's melancholic pride they will pierce.

They are a gentle and violent garden of gods in my new
    landscape.

They will penetrate my midrib to teach me to worship.

And I will find heart-felt family—fond and fierce.

Glamor in Going

★

Kainos
erases
glazes
by phases

Green
cleaned
into gold
gleaned

into gustos
of gules
grace
of garnet

into imago
of burgundy
glaringly
indigo

All days
stay as stasis
that goes
and grays

★

Longevity
leases its longest
freest lief

to the least
jealous
to last

to the generous
enough
to cease

to the gracious
in a great
loss

to the capacious
peace
to not grasp

the gladdest
in time of waste
to be avast

to lavish
leaves
on grave

to receive
the bliss
of grief

caressed
and kissed
by frost

Risk rest
from life
to root fast

Poem for Autumnal Communion
(A poem of praise, or a poem for them who pass away?)

The splashing morning's pluvial rills
Seethe with schools of rusks.
Down from sylvan sanctuaries
They have swum swinging through
The predawn dark
To rest below, each an ark.
Brown or brindled, bristling with rain
But still yet crispy brisk.
One cement street crepitates with these tree-biscuits
And again another stretching onward.
As lamps give way to light of daybreak
Feet come out to meet, hands to make,
The crackers clamour and cry
And change in colour
And consistency.

By noon levigated softened and flattened
To a sprawled slimy polysaccharide flan
In the mazy roads' atlas of pan.

What's after?
Will the bosk-littered blini-batter
Sun-dry to a sacred wafer?

Will deciduous planes and abeles
Have baked that wafer-bread
By earth to be received
(Intinction, it is conceived)
Splattered with wild cordial
From fruits feral
Sharp, sweet and corvine
(Grapes' bird-gut-filtered wine)
Upon this merciless bed
Tortured by so much tread?
Sacrament worthy of elegy
As death
Makes life less
Yet there sings along, a eulogy

For slow breath
That saith
The faith
Slow
Still   low
Yellow
Yes

Wet with Weatherschmertz

As summer bids adieu to the northern temperate zone
it musters this roguish algid monsoon
osmanthus's calliosmic caviar
ginkgo's gamy rimy golden mash
putrid poplar leaves' chocolate smear
pigeons scavenging at autumn's autopsy bash
float inside an inflating aquaballoon

that like a dendritic river grows to infinity
to swaddle in Pluvia's sovereignty
a stray peacock in diminuendo
a field scrawled with sinuous earthworms
flocks winging as if one cried, "Accio!"
chlorophyll desensitized to these parky storms
Changed is the hall, as of eld the repertory

The gods have lost climate control of their ancient garden
to the whimsies of a wanton warden
Niveous numina flummox verdant hearts
Mosquitoes sport sleet; have no cold feet
Fall freezes skeletons to skyr orts
Chill makes uneager bellies ravenous to eat
Snow-sheeted is every wood of Arden

The wastrel warden is purblind to his self-wrought portent
that weather is becoming hard to hent
How many shoots await inclemency
that will give no quarters to treedom
this pending winter of plangency
this despairing dangling daunting time of dark doom?
For this season–sorrow, what species be shent?

A Metereological System

Feathery frondy
deciduous bangs flee from
fall's forward cold front

First Frosted Morn

A late violet
crops up incredulously
blued, slender with chill.

Verna Secunda

Oxalis aureoles both auric and rose
Always abided in our garden.
Today the coelum is cerulean.
They waken from repose.

Dandelions have clenched chatteringly
Their bright neat rosetted teeth.
Today's maw of lawn widens its wreath.
Sun makes merry so caressingly.

Coy, celestial, hued like the deep,
Gazes up the bird's eye.
Easeful and elate Hope is high.
Azure herbs shall not weep.

Nietzsche never preached
To small plants about amor fati.
Today they spring magnanimity
Where sleet blasted and bleached.

Requiem for a Niveous Night in Early November

in the falling rolling grass
of Inner Mongol
which just this noon
was wildflowers'
glorious golddustbowl
roaring with gusty warmth
and sandy mirth
tonight air's breath
is howling with snow

the histie soil is hissing its chill
its sparse hairs have grown hoary cold
a white whirring palsy
has swooped down
on the fleecy fold

Some have grown numb
Some permanently succumb

Every premature blossom of snow
is an untimely bomb

Tonight, cataclysmic crystalline hexagons
retaliate by cumulating tombs

These are not fake flakes

This is our cunningly
bungled climate

Death is come
thrumming its tenebrismic hymn
It is the dead of night
It cannot be more late
Stark earth is starry with brutal beams
Can the deceased in dark injustice
tonight rest in peace?

late night 6th of November

wee hours 7th of November

Topophilia

I'm a wild-reader wonted to walk a bird-hill
Overlooking towers of gold ginkgo foliage
Filleted in fall, when crystalline cerulean winds
Wayfare high like happy waifs, weaving the whiffle
Of leaves as fowls flounder through them rustling
And wrestling with my metronomic steps, which
In a restless boustrophedon have pounded
The path's leaf-litter to pot-pourri poured
Into next year's soil as nourishing spoils—
Boons are what creatures crave and cull from the coddling season:
Those pines with pale pied bark perilously dangling
And peeling at all times are unlocking their cones,
Then lopping them off to the lawn with acids of oblivion—
Epitome of letting go!—where creaking pigeons,
Pugnacious magpies, busybody sparrows, blackbirds
And a brood of brown birds take over, nothing overlooked,
They'll see to it; plum trees wave and waive
Their coppery purple spangles already losing luster
Because thinner crowns' puckered fruit
Are easier to loot; grasses are also dying
Their burly ribbons tawny or violet
As vivid flags to advertise their ripe ears
(I have to say the passementerie is a bit tousled,
Tawdry, even ribald); another kind, whether an orchard tree
I know not, with leaves too pointed for sweet cherry
Anyway, is doing the very same trick with its berries,
Beryl-green, greyish pink, dirty orange, musky maroon,
Swooning into a swarthy puce, delectable (or deluding) hues
For winged wights' grateful use (or a fatal ruse);
I misread the bold foraging tread of birds' feet
For a rude fellow human obtruding on me—
A blunder I joyously repeat, rejoicing to detect
Every time the genuine author of the racket—
All the time pacing and pacing and pacing the place
As if perambulating the glabella or arête of nose
Of a loved face, a fabulously populous face
Enthralling, beside me, such a rambling throng: I trace
Triffid-leaved sycamores drop their three-pronged
Troth-plights throughout the terraced path
And hear birds' claws hop and kiss and keenly press
The paved way with their tricuspate philoglyphs.

Indigo Pond Inversely Pondered

Vast atro-azure waters
Wash affluently and calmly
Round one freckled resplendent pebble
And one pinpoint argent sparkle
Cuttlefish-inked gothic waterweeds
Weave, wind, dance
Their moist-mollified wet-reveried
Mercurial mermaid traceries
To the vibrations
Emanating soundlessly
From the utmost celestial layer
The most exalted exosphere

We nest on the peninsulas or bars
Appropriate to our several ranks
Around bights' bays and high reef-crests
Incendiary chains of buoys
Blink red vigil from banks
Built for navigation and settlement
Fissuring and fenestrating
This liquid obsidian
Pond's large but bounded
And strictly corseted breast

The lapis lazuli pond is cannulated with many inlets
Some disembogue into the indigo
In tacta and clean
(Odorless ghosts with frost-white sheen)
But most tributaries are dreggy and obscene
Tainting and tarnishing the stainless epilimnion

Vibration
Is a surface phenomenon
Libration
Lives deeper above
The drab

Only when the dikē is oblique
Towards obnoxious opacity

Does it turn out to the city
That prodigious pearlescent pebble
Is the luminescent lily-white blossom
(And the silver sparkle, its budding gem)
Of floating *Ottelia acuminata*
They sicken, shrivel and sink dead
When their pond is murky with turbid mud

Smirchless flora
Spiritus alba
Fragile indicator species of the pond
It is poignantly agile to respond
"Native home, indigo pond,
You've caught the contagion
Of caligo. Dear pond, we despond…
O Dis…O Pond…"

Sidereal Paradise

Silver stippled stars, slender sprouts.
Uranic flora germinate in welkin scoured clean.
Bedded and budded, three-night-virgin.

May the faith of firmamental covenants
Never by man be broken.
May Astarte haven these beings in benison.

So that unlike doomed descendants of patented seeds,
These blooms be free to burgeon and brighten,
Not languidly wane early, dim and thin.

May they grow nightly more large, lush and lustrous,
Safe from the smothering of miasmas wan.
From their leucophilic eyes, obviate noisome sin.

Vigilant angels, protect this paradise
From smoggy-smug foul-smelling pandemonium
From modernity's dusty lusts and light pollution.

Song without Words

The supreme song is without words:

only a silhouette against silence,
a presence, an emergence.

Pebbles strung by a snail's silver slime
are track records of his trudgery to rhyme.

All pink tongues in the mouth of a thistle
are sculpted by the slow, circadian chisel.

Led by the moon's cyclical steps
the longeve ocean flows and ebbs.

The clover congregation chant white every May,
clapping triplet hands a beat per day.

The morning glory and the moonflower
March forth each at her dew hour.

Words inked on the page, vibrations etched on tape?
No. Song is time growing inside a living shape.

Ask: what
Is poetry? Answer: a sad and angry consolation.
        —Geoffrey Hill, *The Triumph of Love*

You must praise the mutilated world.
        —Adam Zagajewski, tr. by Clare Cavanagh

If we deny our happiness, resist our satisfaction,
We lessen the importance of their deprivation.
We must risk delight.
We can do without pleasure, but not delight.
Not enjoyment. We must have the
stubbornness
To accept our gladness in the ruthless furnace
Of this world.
        —Jack Gilbert, "A Brief for the Defense"

When a Plane-Tree No Longer Teems

I feel a barrenness in all my bells
That has burrowed through the limb;
I feel its black magic filling up
My leaves to the brim.

Through my many intricate chambers
The sorcerer is slow in coming,
Chilling drafts rustling his dark rags,
Horrible ballads humming.

I've searched for the sly shriveler
In me for three sorrowing years.
My boughs that bore millions of babies
Are now their prebirth biers!

Once words of joy, my exponent leaves
Are now emblems of grief
That the seed-dreaming desire of my soul
Is doomed against relief.

Coveting a Tree, Craving to Climb It

O quince! Albescent androgyne of Queen and Prince!
How you bear your beatific beauty aloof
Alluringly, yet bid me keep at a decent distance!

You lean some white arms on an unattainable roof
And reach others into the unassailable air
And plait the rest into a self-twining woof.

Your demeanour is demure, dignified, debonair,
Letting buzzers bringing your sweet sweat to hives
Sweep your insouciant lovestuff with hair.

Envious of bees dallying at their dizzy dances and dives
Into your flowering flesh's flavorous essence,
To breathe and behold the richer of you, I'll risk lives.

Mountain-Climbing

I pick up a seedpod of acacia tree
Hardened and burnished by time,
And stow it in my trouser pocket.
It makes a tiny ticklish rhyme
When my thigh and shin to walk's rhythm
Are repeatedly straightened and bent—
I hear loquacious trees titter with joy
On their carried ascent!

When the civilians of the field grow lush and lovely and long
While strife-ridden men are discontented or down,
Know that these peaceful will not perdure for long—
Ruthless power rides roughshod over to raze them down.

The comminuted bones can never be remembered—
Dry as sandstorms, they lie gashed and grided and ground;
Will all minutiae of each leaf be meticulously remembered
By roots who've remained to remake the desolate ground?

Melodialgia

As a ubiquitously torrential
Temperament overwhelms
Every distant differential
Niche of all seven realms

As pagoda trees and plantains
Topple like bibulous saints
To delirious skiey inundations
And prostrate like recreants

As the incarnadine Reaper
Doubling as the blazing fiend
Ranges like a crazed vault leaper
Across creek and woodland

As malefic muggy domes smother
The sweeter and more temperate
Than memory moods of Vancouver
And turn street trees desperate

As crisp fructuous meadowgrass
Putrefies and blackens
Under downpours that mass-
Acre nomads' fleecy kins

As one more arboreal idea falls
Into oblivion after hosts

That have let go of the thralls
Of cidal sweltering and frosts

I cannot declaim 'environmental'
In the glare left by felled elms
Euphony turns me mental
Invectives odes and psalms

Hill Greened in Fine Rain

For Geoffrey Hill, the Poet who is the supreme Christian humanist
We humans continue to be human animals, but also uncanny birds,
beasts, plants and elements.

Hierarchies are broken
Tongue's atrocities forgiven
History's heavy sin
Is decomposed by lichen

All the failings that are human
From Adam to Chamberlain
All that nation has bidden
Woefully to betide nation

Decay from lofty pain
Hard and glittering as diamond
To a humble humid substance
Like duff iced with pollen

All the acrid carbon
Coating charred lips of cannon
Has strung new living chains
Inside many a fecund stamen

Every atom of magnesium
That inflicted incandescent burn
As core of chlorophyll beckons
To serene light for strength

There ceases to be any cordon
Barring ren with life's old han
From diverse friendly sovereigns
A billion species of sentience

The rubiginous and sanguine scents
Which contended over the ocean
Of virescent vegetal emotion
Surrender themselves to its silence

All the praxes that are human
Has been gone and revenant
Reverent, equanimous, egalitarian,
To praise the prasios of creation

Wood Song

List, list, list,
The hiss of hœste!
Hear, hear, hear,
The whir of wyrd!

Torn, torn, torn,
Torn of trees torn!
Wa, wa, wa,
Wudu woxen wood!

Boom, boom, boom,
Doom of beam!
Facen, facen, facen,
Fall of feale leaves!

Toll, toll, toll,
Sawol all sawn!
Cearm, cearm, cearm,
Cearcian, coercion ,cearfan!

Wær, wær, war!
Treow tears at terror!
Hear, hear, hear,
Tree's hlow of dreor!

Rue, rue, rue,
Ruin of the rood!
Rān, rān, rān,
Wæl of the wood!

Wierp, wierp, wierp,
Woe is this swipe!
Wail, wail, wail,
Why is this wīte?

Wyrd, wyrd, wyrd,
Wærc's wærword!
Hœste, hœste, hœste,
Wæstm in waste!

Spring Sacrament Sacrileged

I started early—took my pack—
And broke fast on the lawn—
Laid across with bread strips of light—
Fresh appetizers—of dawn—

Noontide's azure angels served
The main course of the flower feast:
Dandelions' golden médaillons
On top of leafy salad tossed

With rainbow grains of cress's white,
Veronica's blue, pansy's purple, sorrel's red,
A chalice of the choicest chlorophyll,
Sakura cream on the side.

And our sweet lord never withholds dessert
Till the banquet had passed its prime:
His buffet let birds, bees and butterflies
Swig buttercups through sunny time.

A swifter puissance than mortal taste
Kept the repast replenished—
It regaled many a reverent guest
Without ever being diminished—

Till one Grendel paid the garden a visit
Grinding gas-powered teeth
And mowed all into his maw before
Time's mellow postprandial scythe.

~~~~~~
~~~~~~

I stroke with an intact hand
The neck of an injured tree,
Hoping the intercession of faithful flesh
Might restore integrity.

I mourn decapitated dandelions,
A meadow of spilled brains;
A wind sifting spectral seeds
Effaces fluffy stains.

Be it by Time's ripe grace and wise
When trees are to go down.
Be every flower free to give up ghost
In self-donned assumption gown.

Dear Black-and-White Kitten I Befriended the Dawn I was in Black Dejection

Were we sent together
for mutual amor and nurture
where this cruel morning
yearningly you sat there?
If it was just a whim
to seat yourself amidst nowhere
thank you all the more
for the comfort and warmth
that reciprocated between you and me,
our twin fortuitous fires.
Your might be silently cravesome,
cold, uncomforted,
sitting needy but staid;
or just biding a rat-raid.
But when I hunkered down, furtively
fondling your ermine fur,
you clove to my clumsy knees
and made intimate innuendoes
that your alacrity to be coddled was acute
that you wished to be stroked sweetly
that you wished to eat.

And that gave me ecstasy
which in turn aroused heat
knowing another lorn creature sought sensual love
from dim, dizzy, disconsolate me.

I had to frisk your sleek coat.
I had to fumble your limber tail.
I had to lock gaze with your large pale gold orbs.
I had to care for you.
Your being had cured something eating me.

So I rummaged my backpack
for a nourishing tidbit.
Not in the noshering habit
of possessing a handy snack,
by heaven's goodwill I happened to carry
a small squarish soft chocolate cake.

It was dark brown, humid, crumbly, like rich, silky loam.
It smelled musky, sexy, sweet.
It smeared on my skin like saccharine earth.
I crumbled crumbs with numb balls of fingers.
You circled my body, you nuzzled me,
you came near a weak waul and curled cumbently, dumbly
you wound sinuously around my
winter-cotton-plumped limbs
and yet seemed chary, decorous, demure, discreet.

Then I tried to break that cake
like a scrannel sacrament, dipped in my chilled sweat.
I reached a bit toward your warm muzzle.
You did welcome, take, and eat.
Leavened baked dough, sweet.
Sugar, cocoa, egg, butter, wheat.

Bit after bit, you received.
And I rejoiced to give.

Warmth from your munching miaow
melted me to melic mood.

Comfort creature, stoke your day's warmth
with this modicum of comfort food.

Make me your

humble servant.

Or better,

accept me

into your feline friarhood.

A Feeling of Felis Felix

As if out of pure faith
You appear, sitting on your hindlegs,
Tail motionless, my fuscuous feline friend
With a pair of bright bronze strands running down
Both sides of your spine
And an aurulent mullion between
The circular celadon panes of your soul.

You stretch toward me
With the precise paw-work
Of a master yogini
And lower your body by my feet.

I fondle your fur like a great
Mud-gold silt-silky African river.
From the muscular bed beneath the smooth strands
My stonecold hand is tingled with heat.
You are rightly a sungod.

Then you lift your forepaws
And tuck them prettily under
Your prone body
A yard away from strewn seeds of cat feed
Brown like roasted grains of wheat.
Excluding the ears alert with bristles
You are a beautifully baked breadloaf
Left on the kitchen board
Gloriously glutting the furry growth
Of glucose-eating golden mold.
O you are never cold.

Pleasure Creature

A tabby tumbles in sun-drenched straw
And grazes on sappy buds of squat shrubs
To give some grass comfort to her gut.
Then, blending with her bed, she naps.

A Blackbird's Burial

Found among scattered rosaries
Of wild strawberry
And bees with flowers they prefer
Loving industriously

Prostrate corpse being pored over
By proletarian pismires
And flies with eyes red as copper
And wings blue as fires

Frangible, flaccid, feathered flesh
No warmer than the curbstone
Not feeling its cheek burning
In the furnace of noon

But for the slight stench of slow decay
Of something once steeped in blood
In my palms rests a speck of pumice
Or rather a sliver of wood

A piece of choicest ebony whose bark
Bears filigreed folial patterns
Almost as if engroved in coal-cerements
Of Anselm Kieffer's fossil ferns

That scarlet sonorous beak
A curtailed, cloven stick
Those trippant tawny legs
Faded, forked taupe twigs
Those eyeballs of extinguished light
Mushy holes of microbial blight

Let the animal made vegetal
By the unmarked, unparsed death
Return rightfully to the embrace
Of the substance of growth

Under the darkly verdant pine
With sunny pins in its hair

Make an indentation in the moist earth
To house against hot air

The sable body whose slacked sinews
Press on the pine's strung root
Lay the heavy brown loam down on
Feather-fronds so light they float

Sweep to a pile the laminae of pine needles
To roof this makeshift mound
Place a pair of cherry leaves on top
To remember the unrenowned

A blithe blackbird hops warbling by
Berries blush in canopies above
Longihorns lounge on roses' thorns
A sapling will suckle this grave

~~~~~~

Serenade

My life has stood—an immured house—
With a hole for nightingale to peek
Latticed with welded iron grille
My unarmed hands cannot break—

In April—May—crowning June—
Brambles and wild briars
Scrambling thick over the aperture
With blossoms soften the bars—

I stand tranquil by the windowsill,
My narrow outlet opened wide
To the blushing rose-spices that
On night breeze sweetly glide.

The roses' layers of scented leaves
Shadily, pallidly shine,
Mirroring the subdued splendor
Of that misty sphere—the moon—
~~~~~~

In the little prairie of my psyche
Grief and gladness grow at peace
Like the ruddy globes of red clovers
With blue plumes of wild peas.

...that plants are singular universals, that is, singular living beings who point toward and, to some extent, encapsulate the universality of life.
—Michael Marder, interview in *LA+:*
Interdisciplinary Journal of Landscape Architecture

For no creature exists that lacks a radiance—be it greenness or seed, buds or beauty. Otherwise it would not be a creature at all. Every being is holy, every being is beautiful, every being is radiant, every being shares a spark of the divine fire.
—Hildegard of Bingen

Trees are sanctuaries. Whoever knows how to speak to them, whoever knows how to listen to them, can learn the truth... A tree says: A kernel is hidden in me, a spark, a thought, I am life from eternal life.
—Hermann Hesse, *Wandering: Notes and Sketches*

The entire creation partakes
Of one ecumenical fare—
It is free and infinitely replenished—
It is simple, limpid air.

Nightingales and roses, woodmen
And tree spirits conspire
One subtle energy dynamized
By leafy folks' green fire.

Nature Comprehends All Things Divine

There is a maple with fronds as fine
As a bird's filaments of feather
Split in flight by winds' flowing combs,
At rest by rays through ether.

Panoplied in pea-green budding leaves
Its perching pose is pavonine:
Sweeping on earth her scintillant train
Of ruddy-gold-pied smaragdine.

When it displays a deep-dazzling blood
Like the ruby red sunset Buddha
Borne on the body of the sacred peacock
It is a sanguine seraphic brooder

Over me, standing under its canopy,
With fevered, fascinated face,
Standing under, yes, but powerless
To understand its puissant grace.

There is a locust with flowers as white
And bright as Gabriel's many wings.
Those in blessed concord move his light;
This tree makes concerted flutterings

Of thousands of papilionaceous flowers,
Each pair of wings under a banner
Pressed and protected, and in turn covering
A keeled boat holding manna;

And when a breeze brushes one loose
From Virgin Mary's green branch,
A pure little butterfly Soul takes flight
Whose faith will never flinch.

Of a sunny morning shining all sapphires
The archangelic form aflower comes;
Against an expanse of heaven's perfect hue
Bees bring hosannas of hums.

Divine spirits still dwell down below
In creation's whole gamut of forms:
Bird people spreading splendid wings,
Sylvan people stretching shady limbs.

But the busy tempo of my sense and thought
Blurs and abridges life's divinity.
For all our cravings for the celestial state
We know not heaven's temporality—

The Prelapsarian time of boundless Eden
Brimming with free-growing flowers
Before a breach of the Earth Covenant
Banished us from its bowers.

The Orchestra of Oros

The blackbirds are our chief syrinx players
With skirling windpipes loud and shrill;
They open the incipient notes of the symphony
When morn's first-light comes to the hill.

Then magpies' larger, longer organs
Join as a second, more sabulous voice.
Their insistence on their sounds' beauty
Does make queer music of creaking noise.

The former two ply their instruments from high
In the canopies of perching trees;
When sparrows enter the harmony
It's from the same altitude as bees.

The sparrows produce dense clattering notes
Thick as eagerly chattering rain;
Their mercurial moods swing their pitch
Across the full score's entire terrain.

Brown finches arrive as antagonists
To sparrows' relentless rhapsody;
Theirs also emanate from the ground level
As a counterpoint, or parody.

Full day is the show time of the chorus,
Birds daintier, plumper, more colourful;
Their arabesquing accents technically require
A sophisticated schooling to warble.

All this while, think you, that plants of the hill,
The woods and wildflowers at their feet
Have listened silently or stood as stones
Insentient and destitute of wit?

Or is the mild matinal murmuration of winds
Through multilayered foliage high and low
Merely the ambiguous mumbling of elements,
A background basso continuo?

Are vegetal beings, with their vivid fingers,
Rather, percussionists?
Tap-tapping tambourines and timpani,
Snapping knuckles of unfurling fists?

The oscine opera is an epiphany of sounds
I'm powerless to compile into words;
The chortles of ichor in cambia and culms
Are only streamed live on akashic records.

Remember Us to Your Mother

—flowers say to me
You shoot up and bloom all across my brainland,
Miraculous ephemeral plants, as after rain
Shoots down like meteors to crater the sand

You splash out green, grow lush and lusty, insane
With the cool moisture's pleasure and plenty,
And glaze vast dunes with rainbow sheen,

When my professor of information technology
Says there are kinds of data that belies or defies
Digitization—like the osmic mythology

Of verbena and primrose in painted lady butterflies'
Minds fluttering as busily as life is brief
In deserts to taste paradise before it dies—

And I feel that only an unworthy, impatient thief
Would go into your presence and leave with a snapshot
Of pixels standing in place of your living leaf,

That he chooses the cheapest of treasures you've got
And flies as if guardian spirits of your dwelling wild
Were speeding in his wake to shoo him out,

So I go out to your homes like an adoring child
To her affectionate mother, just staying there long
And longer, my heart quiet, my thoughts stilled

By your sweetly breathed words, that I belong
With you when I be with you, while you are,
That you believe I will never do a wrong

To your vibrant though evanescent attar
By replacing its ownmost being with anything else,
A symbol, a representation, an avatar,

But if lovingly on paper I paint your precious bells,
Vicariously on a fellow lover they might cast your spells.

Manifestation

If soul is the relation of body to the same body,
Hydrangeas express their genius beautifully.
Azure in acid, incarnadine in alkaline,
Tincture is a function of spiritual state.
Another species has a different expression:
Litmus mingled with potash mutates to indigo
And vinegar dares it to deep dark blood.
Soul imbibes elements wherein body abides
And brings its hue into harmony
By leaving the old soul behind
And leaping into the ongoing flow.

A New Defloration
for gibberellic acid

A tree has no virginity
Chastity or maidenhead
But it can be deflowered
By a potion itself produces
Call it homeopathy
Who could have known
A tree's sacred pharmacy
Could be turned against itself
They have bored holes
In their smooth or ridged boles
There are triturations
Of hulos round the holes
There are sucking bottles
Stuck to them like bolts
We cannot hear it trickle
Into the cambium
Up into branches and twigs
Down into the long suffering
Roots under the cement
The seeding season is past
So there can be no sign
By which to see their flowers
Tiny, many, greeny catkins
Disappear into anywhere

Trees love the wind
For it carries their love
On its omnipresent wings
To wayfare to wander afar
Carries first the semen
The pollen then the fertilized
Seeds to wherever it be
When trees love the wind
Love pervades the atmosphere
Vernalagnia is in the very air
Everyone has tingling skin
And a stirring heart
When trees let the seeds

Of their ample anemophily
Speed on the ethereal way
Or dally and dangle free
Or just rove, lighter than no weight
Because a tree's love knows
No worries cares or woes

But we feel no honour
To stand under
Such confetti of amor
And vivid wonder
We must manipulate matter
And how matter relates to itself
So that vibrations in the souls
Of trees called love or fertility
Are silenced or choked
Trees must stop loving
Because we do not love
How where what and why they love
Because we do not love
To be tickled by vegetal love

We look at a red, red rose
And fancy and flatter ourselves
That the rose loves us
That we so well know
The love of the rich, sweet rose
So let it live but are unkind
To flowers of poplars willows
Because they do not seem
To love us, only the wind

The world is a barbaric barbershop
The Earth inadvertently visits;
Tony gapes his giant craggy grin
And guileless Gaia sits.

He combs through her woodsy entanglements,
He pulls out each sprig's curl;
He rubber-binds her prancing prairies
Into a prim ponytail.

But nothing he does seems a service
To her nonpareil head;
Frustrated, frantic, he shaves her to stubbles—
And finds her stony dead.

~~~~~~

Florists paint this platitude
For infatuated lovers
Over bouquets and nosegays
"Your love gives meaning to flowers."

Already the petals' pages are packed
With passages for bees and butterflies
And won't be made pathetic palimpsests
Overwritten with foreign sighs.
~~~~~~

A Lock of the Earth-Poet

Go and catch a flying curl
Sifted from the salix sylph;
The furred seed, air's purl,
Nimbler than zephyr's self
Eludes your grip
With a little leap.

It is fatuous futility
To flaunt such avarice!
Nature's original agility
Gives with tameless grace.
The grasping quest
Will be unblessed.

With lithe limbs and a quiet mind
Abide long in her bosky bower;
A strand of hair on the light wind
Might light on your page to inspire
An echo of a strain
Of earth's hippocrene.

Phyllomancy

An astonished auspex, I paused outside Room C204
because a pair of black magpies
(smirchlessly swart except for alabaster neckings and rectrices)
swerved, and spoke to me
(light and darkness separate as yolks and whites
by these choice collectors meticulously parted,
contrast more trenchant than any bleached printed page):
"You are celebrating the goldening of plane trees
by gleaning their leaves promiscuously
and improvising scriptures upon them with markers
and pasting them aesthetically on placards.
Do you alter what the venations are sigils for
by thus superimposing your anthropic autographs?
Can you, with inky ideograms scratched
more unartistically than bird-clawed words
in fall's duff or winter's snow, make your meanings
(devout wishes about dubious prospects or despondent loves)
meanings of the leaves? After your yesses comes our no;
for we are a tribe well-tried in gathering reliquiae
who know how densely worded a tree deposits its leaves—
before leafstalks get loose, testimonies are written
thereupon in meta-legible colorful inks
which the elements have mastered to read.
The year's distilled creeds and prophecies:
from plane trees they come, to all life they shall be.
You don't see the poem, but the page isn't empty.
You can't interpolate more, for it's replete.
Or should we say, complete.
So humbly and assiduously we collect them,
they are the body of our nest, as well as its soul.
We live suppliantly within them,
where some time will reveal what they have to tell.
This way, if it be possible,
is how, we believe, you can tell
a plane tree's stories, at all."

Forest Fado

-though you stood inside the life
  that gave you life-
    Brenda Hillman, *"Beneath a Dying Coast Live Oak"*

*Of all the beings that are, perhaps the most difficult to think about are
living creatures, because on the one hand they are in a certain way most
closely akin to us, and on the other separated from our ek-sistent essence
by an abyss.*
    Martin Heidegger, *Letter on Humanism*

...pines   revenant
from livelong   exiles in
obvious oblivion   discerpted
by sable fire   dirge
blazing   sorrowing for
life's   thought

pines spines spicules
painful pins
  -pine's thought
          discalced
yet   panoplied
                in passion
                in -pathy
pines away

        wearing

difficult clearings through
prideful wereminds
        by prickling
          their defunct serotonins
& the pine spirit thins
  the poem it was sickens to thankless dins

what stands serried
inside the viridian
        spicular
              specular
        leaves   thimblefuls   of mirrored

green   first meant
kinesis   inhaled from
          the firmament
          (the verdure's suspiration   stomata clogged
                    grows faint)

stomata oped
so that a sapling   effervesced
          sapid strength   so that
          breath   for all things   succeeding
transpired   throughout   the atmosphere

anemophilous semen
taught all erotic beings
            to   love   wind
(wind   the dryad voice
      has fallen dead
                unnoticed)

swirling resinous seeds
within agile creeks
gymnosperms   (with elder semblable
ferns)   played
with future   freely
      co-authored
      ek-sistential   ecstasy

      (a joy throttled
      in the being that first
      gave it to be)
(the pinebrain   with chagrins
wrinkles   its myriad
            skins)

      these pollenstreams
                are about
          to peter out...
      it seems
the plankton   pinebrain

cannot think   its colorful
branes   into human place
        by osmosis
        symbiosis
        of mater
        with childrace
(that engraved   an abyss)—

        —& again rains its grains
down into old yearned-for friends
standing inside
                        fern-fronds—

—& the sylvan emotion
of the emerald brains
fosters filial life
                        (in all despite! despite!)
by filming it within
fringeless fabulous fronds
unfurling so frolicsomely
from its acephelous
        chlorophyllic   thinking

(the embowerer   the embracer
        itself   is about to sink)

In this obscure life-light they
emanate into campsites where
their biophotons never appear
koanifers will have pined away
Pining inside unmonstrant fate
As ultra-eluctable substrate
A pineforest will have borne ingrates:
Forests of their own souls gave
Those never greet who therefore live
Dendralgia grows; trees come to grief
(With grieving trees all beings sync)

Riddle

after Liz Willis

Which came first, the forest or the library
Which is the mother ,word tree or truth
Beech or Buch
Which birthed which, matter or wood
Sinner or fruit
Who preceded, the redwood or the rood
Which outdures, humanity or sanity
Which way is wider, milky or leafy
What is livelier, vegetus or vita
What is dearer, green or gold
For which do you marry, chrysophilia or virid love

Gaia's Phytopoiesis

A species is an idea
An individual, a text
Each individual is further
Divisible into words
A word is a poem
A poem is a fact
Is something made
A plant is the primal
Maker of ocean
Of air, soil and soul
God makes man
In the image of God
Plant makes its psyche
Whose simulacrum
Impresses entelechy
Into everything alive
Gaia makes plant
Plant makes all
Subsequent
Plant makes
The living world
Or the Earth's
Living worlds
Gaia makes a lobe
The lobe greens the globe
Gaia makes a lone cell
In the image of a leaf
Then the leaf
Believes in limitless life
When anthroprivation
Arrives to ravage
Life word by word
Plants be first rescued
Stowed aboard
Rowed away
Word by word
World by world
In the Arkhive

Genesis

A muse dreams of a myth.
A myth dreams of being born.
Being born, a seed dreams of becoming a tree.
The tree has white water-roots.
The fulgent filaments fatten, pallid in loamless lymph.
Youthful, the skin is membranous and velvety.
Vernal, the green is taut and sleek.
No bulge nor knot has thickened its lanky liquidity.
The tree harbors two buds.
A pair of gems about to germinate.
The tree dreams of a wind to whisper open their lids
To desire and acquire
Everything that be.
Everything that be
Belongs to the tree only.
There is nowhere
A single ray to share.
No competitor nor communal other.
The tree aspires higher and higher
Into empyreal fire.

The gemmae dream of increase.
The increase dreams of release.
The sere season dreams of queenliness.
The solitary old queen dreams of still vanquishing.
Strenuous, her onus must be still sole.
Dolorous, her prowess must be indomitable.
Burdened, bowed, her boughs must be still beautiful.

The sole sovereign falls.
Fatiscent is her fallen body.
Fractured finally into many.
Yet still solitary, without companion, unconsoled.
Dreamless, ungainly, unabsolved.

A solitary tree is a cruel myth.
It is born, when the muse dreams of a crucifix
In a world without hospitality or hospice.

The tree, born and buried in Time's circling stream,
Hears it slowly psalm it to sleep.
Be it to fall alive on a renewed loop,
Will the seed dream of a single tree?

My love, Logos was once solo.
Then the soul lapsed.
Now God makes a seed,
And the seed words a world
Not as a lone stoically-stood rood
But a large limb-laced loquacious jollywood.

I Am the Azurrection and the Leaf

Heard at the vegetal time of dark blue dawning.
There are so many plants inside me
My womb hides a blue translucent wood.

All my mosses and lichens,
Ferns and flowers, trees,
Tremble in a deep well of water.

Their breaths are silent, not quiescent.
I sense their worried susurrus.
I go to them in sleep.

There I become padded into pleated petals.
I have a worm brain and swim home
To the sachet and seal of a furled flower.

There I drown into ancient afterlife
As embryonic arboreal dolphin
Delving in and out of delphiniums.

Into my dream pollen murmurs the tale
Of the first floating blue leaf.
How it began to breathe.

My withered womb. Weak red wreaths.
Blue bacteria. Blue mold. Bluets.
Blue flax. The blue-green bat vine.

The blue matrix of green memory
Is not made up by, but maketh me.

I wish to heal her grief.

Life's liquid lapis lazuli.
The Azurrection. The Leaf.

I live inside worlds of so many plants
That grieve.

Learn to live those griefs.

Dendrogrammatikos/Treeverse

Is what one must con
And be versed in
To be in conversation
With dendros/trees.
Learn every turn
Of each letter in Treescripture.
Comprehend trees common grammar.
Trees vegevolta.
Trees communiverse.

When trees shed shorn of leaf
Do they write sans serif?
Does the vernal verse attach
Verdant tassels of new tagmemes?
Is every lushlovely motion of Life
An outriding foot, a loudblooming Leitmotif?
Do distinct species differ as signifying systems
Or oddly fanciful fonts like Bodoni Ornaments?
What about scribophobic surfaces?
Soiled soils? Murky firmaments?
Do they eradicate erudite elements,
Expurgate filaments persnicketily penned?
Do birch trees write on birchbarks?
Write upon white bark dark marks?
Do buche trees write buchs
On their beechgrey bulwarks?
Do trees write
In oakgalls or with woodpens?
That's O difficult but
Wood of each tree thinks and
Those thinkings are their inks.
Trees write dendrograms.
Subtle grace. Grammatical grains.

Trees write hirsute herringbones
Trees write shy hyphens
Trees write aspiring apostrophes
Trees write stretchy esses
Trees write YYYYYYYYYYY

Trees write atroflagrant A's
Trees write with zigzagging elbows
Trees write fissuring signs of integrals
Trees write aitches to reach into air to mean heavenhair
Trees write cirrous C's
Trees write veggewobbling W's
Trees write aggregates of acuneate asterisks to articulate acute aperçus
Trees write PPPPPPPPPP but don't mean park nor pee
Trees write triffid letters but they're no obituary of tulip trees
Trees write très-trenchant T's to transpierce a piece
Trees write Janus-faced J's upside down
Trees write capital gammas but don't mean gallows
Trees write F's
Trees write f's
(These forms are diFferent)
Trees write infinity signs propped like popsicles
Perfected by winter into icicled twinned quidditch loops
Trees write languages of Hyperboreal Groups
Trees write tier after tapering tier of tildes to tessellate towers
Trees write cursive l's to cut roots curlysnarl
Trees write k's in lowercase to crack and kick clods
Trees write wee e's at the end of their repetend
Eloquent e's
At explosive edges of every tree
Everytree everytree everytree
Tree tree tree
Tree tree tree
Tree tree tree

Is dendrogrammolalia
A pareidolia?

See that tree
Esemplastic of eternities

Eke
Each and every tree
Scribes
In photosentient lines
Its sacred
Treeditional
Kabbalah

Its simple
Infinite
Enigma
Tree

Tree tree tree
Tree tree tree
Tree

Written in Wood

inspired by Aria Aber & the VS Team

"All earthlings should write memoirs
So that life's traces are made accountable.
Everyone should be amanuensis of her own memory
That loved ones coming later could read.
Do not open this Book of My Story till I have gone
Till I have gone on, till I have gone across and beyond.
I would have lived thus that you will accept my word,
My flesh in ruins, as our final and faithful bond."

I revel in this exuberant, exhilarating melée of voices
Walking between rows of proud plane trees
With boles sturdier than pillars of Pompeii once were
And branches that have made their ways
Not without hurt, not without repulse,
Through the convoluted spaces of the civilized sky
And think, Everything that I can covet to know
About a tree is already written in wood.

It is an apt miracle how the sylvan people
Live through suns and breezes, droughts and floods,
Receive kindnesses from birds and bees,
Bear the belligerence of human hegemony,
And meticulously record every lived moment
In the architexture of their woody monuments,
In the burs in the heartwood, watermarks
In the alburnum, rough ridges and trenches
Riven by slow insistence into thickened bark,
In the varying density and differing shade
Of the wood, in the little snarls of sinew
Grown back as scars after severances,
The outermost skins that peel off constantly
But not without having carved their shapes
On the underlying layer, their successors.
How every tree is both the body and its soul,
Both the present and its past, being
And memory, memoirist and memoir,
How oracular this is. And I gasp to recall
Those giant sequoias of the American Southwest

With their vast cylindrical pages stacked
To such prodigious volumes in a thousand years
Standing in misty mountains, ancient, wise,
A sacrosanct living library of every happening
That once transpired through heaven and earth,
Laid rudely open by late liberalist capitalism
And all the scrolls, tablets and codices
Exposed, vulnerable, raw, red, letters bleeding,
And then gone up in a reckless holocaust
To fuel fast furious comforts of modernity.
Horrible way to die and be read. Yet when aging
Is gradual and graceful, when the perishing,
The passing away, is unforced and unhurried,
When they decide to leave their bodies behind
When their time has come to depart, and let
All the pollen they have strewn, seeds sown,
Animal companions entertained and fed,
Fungi nourished, other plants harboured and nursed
Carry life on for them in the next eternity,
What happens to those volumes of wood?
Certainly ligneous matter will decay.
There is no perpetual preservation of Final Truth.

But even more apt, more miraculous is how,
And this is the most loving and lovable about trees,
Dryadic memoirs go on writing themselves
Even after their memoirists have bade farewell.
They rewrite their sacred pages as a means
Of being rightly read. They open up to perusal
And revision by mites, worms, beetles, fairy stools,
Mosses and lichens, saprogenic orchids,
Who slowly knock upon the library door
And are admitted calmly at due time
To browse and take the abundant teachings
And add reverent footnotes, marginalia, commentaries.

When writing a memoir, men and women ruminate,
Why should I give my bounty to the dead?
Trees, as they leave testimonies and travel on,
Dead to this world, give their bounty to the living.

Plants' Turn

for Ada Limón, Franny Choi and Danez Smith

Which world would you prefer—the one we have here
And now, where humans are the only species
Who has the right to world, or one in which
The plants, the meek, the poor in soul (or, as Heidegger has it,
The poor in world), not only inherit the earth
But also the world? Would you tell their stories
Speculating about their passive stocks and veins,
Or listen to their long-silenced eloquence swell,
Your own voice irrevocably quelled, yet content
With your ignorance? After millennia of suppressing
Photosynthetic species as unspeaking, subaltern,
Would you surrender to plants their turn?
When speculative philosophers say "the plant turn"
They hope for redirection of theory's own discourse,
But let us attend to this subtle sibilation of terms
Neglected like lichen, small as moss:
The plants' turn comes when it is the plants
Who come with their own faces and phrases,
Their lives and selves, to turn to us,
And tell us, teach us, about them—and us.

An Armistice of the Elements

1 The Advent of the Torch
The stupendous sculpture of the snowflake
Is suspended aloft, aslant. Its center,
A hexagonal hollow, longs to take
Fire into its embrace. At a canter,
The torchbearer ascends to the altar,
Rutilant light lapping the pale blue shine
Of water crystal, or its avatar.
Winter Olympics opening: the compline
Is this amalgamation, or armistice
Of gelid water and fast fervid fire.
Real flames surrounded by symbolic ice
Rhythmically decorously suspire.
From skull and crossbones can sprout a gay leaf;
Fire's rage makes truce with icy calm of grief.

2 Six Branches to Bring Consummation
The monumental snowflake is not just
Torchbearer, but olive-bearer. Leaves sprout
From six cusps. Shapely symmetry, fair and just
As green spring from white winter coming out.
It's all ice-blue, but fancy can envision
The branches painted olivaceous green.
Green roots in earth but has airy vision,
A uniter of uranic and chthonian.
Making peace with stolid earth and lithe air,
A grove grown from the song of ice and fire
Stands in place to cut elemental war
Short, while long lives its uncut lush hair,
Memento of amity of fire, water, air, earth:
Verdure is creation's consummate mirth.

They literally breathe us into being. All cultures turn
around plants' metabolic rhythms. Plants are the substance,
substrate, scaffolding, symbol, sign, and sustenance of
political economies the world over. We must learn how to
work with and for the plants so that we can be nourished
and clothed and sheltered and pleasured and healed—
without destroying the earth. These are the world-makers
we need to heed if we hope to grow livable worlds. And
our worlds will only be livable worlds when people learn
how to conspire with the plants.
 —Natasha Myers, "How to Grow Livable Worlds: Ten
  Not-So-Easy Steps"

The Year Earth Sang Encomia to Humans'
Epicedial Metanoia

for Sir David Attenborough & his
affecting narrative The Year Earth
Changed

In the incipience of the year two thousand and twenty Anno
    Domini
humans' planetary empire tremors at an end.

There is a dysrhythmia that palpitates in lethal infectivity. A
    pandemic pulmonia.
Medical Messiah is not in the offing.

The nostrum is for gregarious humans to go into hermetic hiding
and cease to be garrulously globetrotting.

When footfall goes unfallen, din disappears, mephitic metabolism
    is arrested,
the human leviathan pules in privation.

When boulevards, beach resorts, luxury workshop for venatic arts
lie in post-apocalyptic vacuity and peace,

When smudgy perspiration rilling down urban trudgers' shins dry
and those shins revert to the country,

When the egregiously flagitious, direly strepitous worlding of man
    is bereaved
Earth is respited and breathes.

Alaska's coniferous littorals listen in for humpback whales
rediscovering their chorales;

A cheetah chirp-chirrups from a gashed gazelle, alert, a capella, wee,
and her cubs cavort felicitously to feed;

Sika deer now flourish on ancestral herblore in sharded meads
weaned from bran crackers and plastic;

Proud parenting jackass penguins are pullulating with plump chicks, their fishing lots unoccluded by ochlomachies;

Loggerhead turtles' lucently glazed eggs gloriously hatch in untrod
    dunes,
ebon babies blink sabulous beads;

A taupe alba-crested rotund sparrow gauges the deserted Golden
    Gate Bridge
and renovates her long untried love-lay;

A pining puma prowls the municipal and banquets in brash daylight
basking in bohemian bonhomie;

When laid-off men and women plant food for village-vandalizing
    elephants,
elephants feast docilely in their rightful paddies;

When plantains and incense and mantras sanctify ripening wild rice
elephants desist from human sacrifice;

In India the androgynous Buddha smiles in Nelumbo nucifera asana
as turbid Ganges relearns aery limpiditas;

Anshul jubilates at miraculous Himalayas materializing out of miasma:
"Vile vapors pent up a parousia!"

When world economy is uneasily lulled to sleep by an eschatological
    epicedium
Earth ecstatically reawakes;

When humans' tread retreats to mandatory claustration in locked
    dens
lemon verbena and bees frisk as in Eden;

Is it paranoia to interpret the corona's carols as a grief for joy
since nonhumans grow lush from capitalism's fat grave?

How should those who unwillingly precipitated this charity hear
    these encomia
of the reluctant experiments of metanoia?

How should gregarious humans tread back when grief abates?

How greet the exuberant Earth?
How greet the eirenic Earth?
How greet the eleutheric Earth?
How greet the esperant Earth?

With some astounded glee,
        some atoning ruth,
            some awakening hiraeth,
                some abstemious faith.

Witnessing Tree Trauma, July 20th, 2021
(P is for both plane and pain)

This body towers like a T
What body waves like a W
T is for both tree and trauma
W is for both woods and wounds

My pinksmooth balls of fingers weep to
Be wetted by a
Bit of hygrophanous
Cambial bark
Green supernovae ex-
Plode into unripe
Strawberry gold seeds
Each bristle
Bursting with bathmist green

A ravished/ravaged ramus
Swishes/swooshes through the
Ishishishishish air
Cacumen-first
(When the swooning cacumen
Reels near the ground
The green quiver of curlicue
§
  §
    §
      §
Crepitates
Like hkrkkkhrkhrkkkhakenkreuzzzz
Collapses
Crashes
F L A T)

For the dun hue of his costume
A man was not seen
But he is seen now
To be high up trussed to tree
Twining khaki trews
With crackling tree

His flamingly back-&-forth handsaw
Is creaking & crazing
As if
Treacherous lover
Jugulating lover
Dominant love
Dementing & destroying love

Tree inhales carbon
From his stertorous exhalation
He inhales oxygen
From tree's bliss-blitzed being
Breathing Earthing eating
(Together) (man with tree)
But this is not a con-spira-cy
With
This is a conspiracy
Against
Tree
{{{{{treechery}}}}}

Brachium after brachium
Is breached
Gyrates about the point
Of last breaking
Blunders bibulously
Down
Under
Chlorophyllous debris
Amid brazen boutades of
Abominable bombination
Of the electrically-brawned
Rubiginously-fanged
Blood-Axe

On the blasted
Boulevard
Boughbecks have bled
Into boundless waves of ocean
Who says mutilated trees are mute
Who says hewn trees hemorrhage unseen
Hear

WWWWWWWWTRTRTRTRWHWH
PLKTPWRTHRRRWWWKTTTTT
See
Treegore is treerheum is treeslaver is treeriver
From the rift of incision/intrusion disemboguing into
Ishishishishish air
The blade interpellates
Golden prana plashes all over
Wafted/whirred as wooden sand

(Demarcation of Life & Riven is repand)

Man tromps through downed foliage
Man tromps through truncated trunk-trash
Man tromps through aboveground tumulus
Man tromps through crumbs of disintegrated trombones
Man tromps through clarts of disjointed treebones

P is for both prayer and prey
T is for both temenos and tomb
W is for both wisdom and wiped out

What
Is the aftermath of
This macabre plant-dance
What
Is the aftermath of
PTTSD
(Post-Tree-Trauma Stress Disorder)
Attenuation of shade
Blazing gaze through glade
A sap-stained wade

Is P for pandemonium
Is T for tenuation
Is W for waste

We War Briefly upon This Earth

Dramatis Personae
(In order of appearance)

Celestia, Beaming — Thalatta, Tumultuous
Thalatta, In Peace — Littora, Awakening
Littora, Aslumber — Sylvia, Intruded
Sylvia, On the Plain — Oread, Remote and Insuperable
Oread, Forested — Man, In the Aftermath
Celestia, Glowering — Mediatrix, Montanus
Man, In Extremis

Celestia   Before everything there was nothing,
Nothing but bright nothings.

Thalatta   Before the brevity of eternity is enacted
My glaucous length will have rested many a decubitus.

Littora   I was the eldest of Land and Ocean;
Yet I am born and reborn with their every motion.
Wherever she and she heave bodies to embrace
I quietly arise, as a pearly wavy edge of lace.
This instant ,she and she are becalmed with repose.
So I wait to waken and live, when they again move.

Sylvia   I am a verdant virgin and consort to Oread.
My brown loamy meat is her flesh;
My limestone bones join with her diaphyses;
Her pure antiseptic lymph purls in my veins.
From these my ecstatic excrescences spring,
Those parts of immortal charm and remembrance,
My luxuriant hair. Each tress trees, proud, erect, robust,
Nutating, cachinnating, alimenting, riding on free gusts.

Oread   I am a handsome and sturdy female.
I am as tall as I am deep, as wide as I am varied.
I enwomb many viscerae and expose many terrains.
I am bony ;I am chubby; I am pubescent or shaggy.
More than four fluids course through me,
Sluggish or swift. I run, first a cone, then a prism,
Then a frustum, a mesa, then a broken blue tooth,
Then my vibrancy trembles into sharp splinters.
Yet however jaggy or slippery I become, never treachery.
Sylvia's fidelity metamorphoses but will never change.

Celestia   After bright nothings there enlarges a dark something.

Then my serene eyes grow seared with too many shadows.
Irises, cornea, conjunctivae, retina, all delicate clarities
One dense and indistinct amaurosis.

Man   What is this thing? What am I unbecoming?

Thalatta   Then sparks and shrapnel and shattering screams
Slash my peace into seething shreds.
Prodigious rigid birds plunge like meteors
Moveless in their deadly speed,
And my saline aquacity douses all hot velocity.
I do not taste scorched feathers or singed meat.
A mephitic tang of molten metal greets.

Littora   What is this scene? Has a new scene dawned?
Why does dawn come yet Heaven mourn, so dim?
Why does combusting Man lunge over my thinness
Onto an element I did not know, Land, my one mother,
Has grayed and hardened to? Am I born into Allocene?
I sense the confusion and despair of calamity.

Sylvia   I can no longer behold myself
In its erstwhile lucid beautiful details.
I am seeing all caliginous umbrage and lutulent mist.
My myriad species are lost in a mere looming gloom.
I am distanced from me. I am bereaved. I fear to see me.
Horripilation. Something that should not be is upon me.

Oread   I am made a barrier. Or am I?
I gain incipient knowledge of my other side.
Optical art works to transform me from bulwark to bar.
I am not intimate. Not amiable. I stand off far.

Man   My right hand rends the left;
My right eye vies with its brother
To gouge it out so it ceases to bother;
My body and soul grow impatient of mutual gift;
Each part yearns for internecine theft.
Inside the somatic and the mechanic wrest
Blood from the soft and shards from hard.
Pain, pain, pain! Agony has detonated.
The impetus that hurtled me all the way along
Pelts me hard on this shore so far-flung.
Mountain, woods, sky, sea: amorphous and alien.
Icy chill and hostile strangeness hem me in.
That mountain, sable, frore with soot-black snow

I must conquer to reach safety, I have all wherewithal.
Where is the pass? There must be some way through.
Even if I have to slay my way as I always slew.

Celestia   Sylvia! Serenade me to salving sleep!
Chant a wild text to me, for I am given a shot of nightshade.
I am at some lyke wake. Come! Assuage! Allay!

Thalatta   All my violet and turquoise fronds
Have turned affrighted scarlet at Man's scent.
Celestia! Oread! Are you higher up cognizant!
Celestia & Oread   Yes!

Littora   Ocean! Thalatta! My Mother!
Oread! Land! My Mother! An opalescent sheen
Is upon my body. It flecks flickers and flinches.
What malady afflicts me?
What is this ominous Other?

Sylvia   Acrid carbonization has charred and choked my
    trees
My tresses. My sussrrus is sputtering with powder.
The sound is not pulchritudinous. I cannot melody.
In such a brief forever, I forfeit such memories!
Wounds ooze a sick thick booze from breached wood.
I spatter sap across acres of roods. My own blood burns.
Is there no remedy? Pray, Celestia. You clairvoyant!

Celestia & Thalatta   We cannot but see Man,
With all our puissant Seeing.

Oread & Littora   We cannot stop the echolalia
Of Man's deafening cacophony.

Sylvia   Soft! (though Man will not be soft)
I hear a sober singer in my omphalos.
Whose form is solemn and somber.

Mediatrix   Celestia!
                   Thalatta!
                   Littora!
                   Sylvia!
                   Oread!
Survival of Man who blew himself up to your trauma
Needs a pass you might withhold.
Will your united stronghold punish his crime
By swallowing him up in your claustral fold?

Celestia, Thalatta, Littora, Sylvia & Oread *(Tutti)*
   The arsonist
Will have to save, not exterminate, himself,
If we are to minister to our communal weal.

Mediatrix   Man!
What do you feel? Wrath or grief?
Retribution or remorse? What do you crave?
Reconciliation or short reprieve?
What life do you envisage, if miraculous charity
Ever escorts you out of this region's algid apathy?

Man   You might exact all you want,
Whoever calls out to me. I wish only to be rescued.
On whatever terms you propose. I am penitent,
However I might have sinned.
Will you guide me through?

Mediatrix   I will bear your words to those
Who will only decide your fate. Celestia, she who beams above,
Thalatta, the nymph of aquamarine, Littora, daughter of limen,
Sylvia, the most vigorous, virid and svelte sylph,
And Oread the athletic maid. They shall appraise your faith.
They only compose the wild text you will or will not read.
They may issue an injunction or graciously lead.
Celestia!
Thalatta!
Littora!
Sylvia!
Oread!
Pray hear the worth that Man says he has.

Celestia, Thalatta, Littora, Sylvia & Oread *(Tutti)*
   Man shall war no more
With himself or, that is the true mandate, with us.
After some time, he shall find what then will not be
Necessary for us to illuminate. During the term,
Let him dwell with us. He shall learn.
Learn the tristesse of everything Man-torn.
We will receive faith as what is grown
Where he has to grow, not what is forsworn.

Mediatrix   Man!
Listen!

Man   Amen. Amen. Amen.

Accurst be your damned doomsday plan!

Seed Song

for Patricia Westerford & her overstory

Most human kinsfolk conceptually impair trees.
Hard of hearing, I began early to hear trees.

I made fairies of holly leaves, acorns, pinecones,
Walnuts and Kentucky coffee pods live near trees.

My father taught my mind with mysteries of cambium,
Chlorophyll and synchronous bloom to revere trees.

He showed the feats of ash, elm, hornbeam, queenly beech,
Oak, sycamore, hickory and tropics' queer trees.

He gave me Ovid chanting feral verdant tales
About outlandish gods turned to familiar trees.

His death compressed my alburnum to duramen.
Forestry schools I went to would commandeer trees.

I swinked bagging wild Indiana maples' breaths.
I grieved the garish blight on those belvedere trees.

Gaseous chromatography worded wind and howled,
"Gregarious, altruistic, socially aware trees!"

"Hurt, blow molecules onto airborne marathons,
They procure time against more attacks for peer trees."

Brief public awe at threat-bruiting bosques was ensued
By doubt and derision. They're, after all, mere trees.

I became a dendrophone futilely rousing
Godless humans to golden gospel: beware trees.

Godforsaken days; I ate nuciferous groves.
Amanita would ease my shedding like sere trees.

Poison I did not partake, yet. Sempervirens,
Aspens, Lily, Douglas fir. Many a year, trees.

I strayed, resurrected,scienced green, learned to love
With estranged pain men to whom nought could endear trees.

Wrote of wisdom and salvation of the sylvan,
Fragile, fabulously varied volunteer trees.

Yggdrasil and Old Tjikko abreast with Rumi's
Everywhen-nowhere Love stand as seer trees.

Nursed pages of prose as if numinous poetry
Circumnutated there like young maidenhair trees.

Got read by geeks, nomads, millionaires, tree-sitters,
Paralytics. Wondrous sales, woe of martyr trees.

Witnessed in a feckless court to a forest's right
To stay whole, give slow, keep from any sawyer, trees.

Was anguished by news of lovely humans who got
Flare-fleshed by freddies cleaving to Douglas fir trees.

Grew old in a warming world whose mad heat had been
Making massively headily disappear trees.

Built a high-tech-cooled hospice or ark in Front Range
For kapoks, bruyère, Lecythis, sepetir trees.

Home Repair craved a keynote on how green heals future.
Why would they invite me but not summiteer trees?

Maytenus, Syzygium, Ziziphus I showed them.
Ichor of Tachigali versicolor trees.

Plant-Patty has her seed set, ready to suicide.
Drinks. Swirls like winged seeds. Vivid, leafy. To hear trees.

Conversation on a Transplantation

"Mom, I have to enlist your help. The brawny bathmism of this
Sansevieria trifasciata has breached its pot.
The porcelain is broken in twain. We must transplant
This brave darling into something larger." Mom rises, groggy
With sleep. "Lucie, you can't empty it out like this.
It's clinging too tight. Break it with a hammer."
Lucie lets the heavy hammer-beak nibble at the edge
Tentatively. The shattering noise isn't timid.
A shard bounces hard against the opposite pane of glass,
Lands explosively several yards away. "What are you
Thinking about? You've got to lay it on its side.
Hammer its lateral side. That way it'll fracture
Into big, neat chunks." "This way? Right! Here we go.
Ouch! My finger. A tiny chip's fillip." "Whaaaaaaaat?! What
Did I tell you? Get off! What if you get tetanus?
And what if a sharp shrapnel slaps you in the eye?"
"I'll go rinse it. Apply iodine. Look, this isn't tricky work.
I've scooped out the soil. Just place the root ball
In the large pot, fill the earth back in, ram it firm,
And water thoroughly. It's okay!" When Lucie hunkers down
Beside Mom with her two minute slits trimly silenced
From haemorrhage, Mom isn't pleased, or
Appeased. "What did I tell you?Must you meddle
With all this perilous lark? Why must I? If I got my way this'd
Have found its way out of the house. Been thrown
Out. Whoever takes a fancy to it they're welcome to it.
I'd wash my hands clean of this thing. Transplant! As if
This pot had done me any service anyway!
Then must I let it sever your fingers?"
"You've inhaled its oxygen!" "It's breathed my carbon! What?"
Lucie's heart turns clamorous against rain. Her face
Begins to rain. "This is a tropical species! It'll perish
Miserably outside in winter chill! Also do not expect
Anyone'll exercise the eleemosynary volition
To take it in. It'd be bound for demise! How can you
Say such a diabolical thing or even entertain
Such a notion, mom?" "Don't undertake an act you aren't
Adequate to. Stop weeping. I hate it." Her tone is something
    ironical

Something cold. There's an angry astringent heartbreak
In it. There are several things broken. The pot. The skin.
The maternal-filial covenant. Love me love my green symbiont.
The green isn't mine. Love me love all I love. All I live with.
Love green better than you love me because I
Love photosynthetic beings far better than I can
Any member of the sneaky self-absorbed Homo.
Not sapiens. No sapience if you cower at a little thimbleful
Of scarlet innocent blood. If a plant can breach its stronghold
Then some accident too can breach my skin. No fuss.
"You know well how blasé people trash puppies
When they somewhat fall from favour. Irresponsible?
It's an iniquity. And what you'd do is idem. Idem. Do you
Know what idem—" "I'm not talking about abandoning,
I'm having in mind perhaps some far better gardener
Might offer it a home." "You know this is argument
For argument's sake. And I know it." Lucie is raining
Rheum riotously. Lucie is a pluvial planet. Lucie's orbs
Roll away to calm down so their ebullient water will cool to ice.
"Did you," Lucie feebly accosts Mom, having quieted
And quelled her raging grief, "get this Sansevieria
From a friend as a gift?" Enlisting memory as remedy.
"No," Mom is brisk, brusque. ,"I bought it for ten bucks."
Then relenting a fraction of a faraday, "I got from Gina
Those pendent lilies." "So that's about it, our gift plants?"
"Right." Mom would like to pay an homage,
But hushes, hesitates, because, how?
"Isn't it wondrous that it's actually grown five times
In amplitude and magnificence since your ten bucks?
Haven't you developed an affective bond?"
Lucie's atmosphere is Favonian with fatigue.
"It is good that it has done well. Lucie, I was wild.
That was mad language. I'd keep it. At any rate."
"I am happy you concede so much." Arch, not unkind.
Lucie hovers patiently above the expanded home
To pour out the housewarming libation. Mom tidies up.
"You know what that throwing out thought called up?"
"Nope. What?" "When I was a naughty baby Gran Peggy
Threatened to defenestrate me, and you were
Sorely injured, sorrowing, outraged. At her callousness."
"Oh!" Mom halts her work. ,"That serious?"
"It's idem." More pensive, less passionate, a whit wistful.

"But if I part with a closet, an old armchair, you won't care?"
"I'm always alright with ditching things. Things are,
After all, things." Lucie gazes lovingly at the winsome,
Glaive-like foliage in ameliorated accommodation.
"But what you forgot about is that a green plant,
Greenly growing, exceeds thinghood." "Yes." There's
Confused compunction in Mom's comportment.
"But don't forget I love. You." The plant is planted well.
By Mom. Her hand working the spade is steady and true.
"Yes. Love, a gambit. Green is generous. I forgive you."

Two Poems from a Tree-Climber,
No Ascender above Trees

Scansion
I make a sanguineous sgraffito
of skin on my limb
which slips fricatively from
the limb it scrambles to climb

The chastisement isn't a blood myth
that tree and man must war
When the scarlet browns to scar
it's a tattoo of a wood bur

This sakura tree's spared boughs
(debranched like Moore's Poetry)
eject me from wounded meaning
deny me dendrometry

Its surviving lianas lick weeping
wood-eyes created by pain
ringed with time, rimmed with amber
and forbid me to scan

But bark of the cherry has pierced
the epidermis trying to read
On the keenly tingling thigh
a kinship is inscribed to bleed

A Return to the Native Arbor
a wiry puny wildly
tremoring anxiously
adhibiting thing wraps
itself around a vilely diminished
beloved being
a prolific life by force
flensed is so difficult
to hug with all but
all embraceable wood
slashed off stripped away
in the portable recorder

a testimony to changed arborrain:
here I am again finally
after all the mayhem
all the havoc
up in my old cherry tree
again my old cherry tree
as in my family
after bruising my foot soles
my knees and my thighs
I finally have managed
to scramble up into the tree
house the tree as house
the house in the shape of the tree
now I am joining
in a cutaneous communion with the tree
together with all the ants
scampering up and down
the crumpled bark of this
wondrous tree equilibrated
very precariously grappling
with my own weight grasping
the bulk of this supporting
life giving life sustaining tree
now I can hear it breathe
I can hear it pulse
only because finally
I found my way to depend upon it
to get into it after all the injuries
and crippling mutilations done to it
after all the amputations
and violent loppings
and carnages people have wreaked to it
  still I am here still
  I am here insisting
  I have an intact family

Guerrilla Gardening

They demolished the cafeteria. Land lay in waste.
It was spring. Sandstorms swiped the loosened soil
Into the taupe sky. Spring showers fell in muddy drops.
Smell of petrichor. Sniff the fluid soul of earth
Gladly, gratefully moist. When the veins of earth
Quickened green sprouts shot forth,
Alfalfa, abutilon, erigeron. Hardy plants, grits were
Grist to their mill. Then dandelions landed,
And plantains, cresses, grasses. Goosefoots
Planted their feet. Willow saplings swayed
In May's hot winds. Tiny paulownia seeds
Broke crusts of dirt, had growth spurts. Stems
Towering over my head and thick as my wrists.
Hairy leaves larger than my oversized summer shirt.
May gone. June past. In the interval
Green-thumbed retired couples had cleared plats
And planted summer salads. Lettuce, cabbage, kale.
We waded into the quick-growth groves
To discover spent packets of veggie seeds
Discarded alongside withered weeds exhumed
From hastily hoed beds. Cultivation always
Knows how to wedge its way into the wild.

London planes, privets and palms followed
The pioneer trees who growing in the vanguard had
Gardened the rupestral bed with their rhizomes
Created compost and comfortable microclimates
By sending up swift solascutums. Under their aegis
As if by virtue of a floral fairy vagarian votively
Working the land, a wondrously various
Voluptuous wildflower garden began to germinate
In the verdant vault's velutinous viscid light.
Red clover and white, blue bird's eye, pale purplish aster,
Squat thistles with brownish pink prickleheads,
Wild carrot's flat meal saucers with cranberry
Dotting the centre, hollyhocks hotly blooming,
Wild strawberry and grape blooming plain green
Then coming out with blood-bright gaudy fruit:
With few people's heed, without signing deeds,

Some fugitive had found this field and secretly
Made it its garden. We did not know or see
Its face. We never heard its voice save in the wirbling
Of winds, nor smelled its odour except
When the flowers themselves taletattled
About their whimsical caretaker.
This wild garden of profuse herbs and hardy trees
Had glades in its midst, where human forms
Mingle their shadows with the garden fairy's green shade.
They tended to rows of delicious leafy greens.
The cabbage heads looked like meek unmoving sheep
With folds of fronds for fleece. Through the summer
We saw them peacefully at pasture, guarded
(Or gardened) by their herbherds. The wild gardener
Protected its plants in shapes of pollen-plump bees,
Long-tailed butterflies, hummingbird moths on blurry wings,
Birds bringing on timely rain and cats negotiating
With the sun for just the right light and heat.
September saw both the wild and the cultivated
Fractions of the land flourishing in full fanfare.
In fall, word came that we would have to fight a war.

It had been waged. The gauntlet was laid.
What they willfully misunderstood as a
"Vacant" lot was to be reclaimed to
A cement meadow! And rows of limousines
Were to graze on it, roaming and ruminating,
Emitting chugging noise and acrid gas,
Coming to rest in a standing sleep.
A parking lot! A grey, gaunt, lifeless land
Where those oil-guzzlers could roost
From whence they could go prowling, polluting,
Pullulating! Surely such vivacious gardens
As ours should never be swallowed up
By such villainy. We must vindicate our viridaria
Against man's wanton vitiating will. We must.
We devised a tactic. We would mobilize
Mobs of venefic flora to fight a guerrilla war.

Determined to deter invaders with datura,
With its venom saturated sap and seeds,
We ventured into the mountains to collect forces,

To gather an army of this deadly flower.
If the archangels of the carpark saw their knotted stocks,
Pale pendulous purple trumpets and fanged fruit,
They would read the bruit, baulk ,and back down,
Leaving the garden unblighted by the blasphemy of cement.

We were holding packets of vegetal myrmidons
In our hands. In late September's last warm showers
We planted them in the field, giving them
To the moist willing mud. Increase and multiply.
Militate against their imminent crime.
We scattered them, muttering encouraging mantras.
Give me to believe that you have a seed
And I shall expect great miracles

The jimsonweeds prospered like weedy street kids
In dingy green tatters, all their hardscrabble
Life's earnings clattering in thorn apples
They tucked high up inside flaring white sleeves
Stained with the squalid lilac of cheap waterish wine
Imbibed to cheer their battered spirits.
They stood amid other plants, wiry-sinewed, wary-eyed,
With Thérèse Defarge's malign calm in their meagre mien,
Vigilantes with quiverfuls of bitter poison
Inculcated by the iniquities of life. Why should jimsonweeds
Or any weeds render up their dwelling-place to limousines?
They occupied the avant-garden, guerrilla warriors
In green guise, holding their grenades against gruesome guilt.

Yet what chance did wanchancy weeds stand
Against man and his machines? An ominously grey
October afternoon, grey cement walmed from
A mixing cylinder and overwhelmed all.
This was the final guerdon of four months'
Guarding and gardening against all odds.

The whey-grey vomit of the cement van hardened.
A few attempts by goosefoot to wedge a limp toe
Or a bony knuckle into a crack in the concrete
Have been all our consolation that some presence
Continued to guerrilla-garden in the gap.

6

The Sweet Gean Saga

What we love   How we care for it
Is where we live
        —Brian Teare, *Companion Grasses*

The Sweet Gean Saga

1

Should I rest complacent, satisfied
That I know the Gean through and through
If I discover that it's classified,
Videlicet Carl Linnaeus, in the Eu-
Karyota, the Strepto-, Embryo-,
Tracheo-, Spermatophyta, the Mag-
Noliopsida, the Mesangio-
Spermae, the eudicotyledons, the G-
Unneridae, the Pentapetalae,
The rosids, fabids, Rosales, the Ros-
Aceae, the Amygdaloideae,
The Amygdaleae, the Prunus?

Does that scholarly tally tell the lineage
Of this flowerchildren's branchy hermitage?

2
Of this flowerchildren's branchy hermitage
In a pocket greenspace at the imperious heel
Of a condominium tenanted by tartars in dotage—
A tree, a sonsy cherry, with an ommatidia soul—

I can say much, and much more. That its stature
Is what Parthenon would be; that the bole bifurcates
At the height of my groin, poising the outreacher
Boughs horizontally parallel, unbowed by sweet whites,

Rounded, untaperingly robust in sustained length,
One carrying your feet, supporting your hands the other
As a handlebar, two-tiered bridge of supple strength,
Cispontine cherry trunk, trans laced with a slim acer;

That two limbs of stout girths rear steeply upright
With elbows I fold my limbs in like a stylite.

3

In steep elbows I fold my limbs like a stylite,
Watching my domicile's skeletons flourish.
A tree is a living house that self-strips in the night
Boreal, and decks anew when breezes are beamish.

Manysouled Gean is a springtime scriptorium
Of maroon smoothsmall brush tips green-dipped
And disheveled by warmth to limn anthograms:
White, whiff, bee, bloom, a polysemy of script.

I, grey querier among human facades' accidie,
Clamber up to read such vivid vernal yesses
That my child's sad malady blurts out merry melody
As cherryanthemums dehisce, eclose, recrudesce!

The Gean's body is fragrant with froth, furred by moss.
I scramble raptly. Yet blossom is gravid with loss.

4

I scramble madly for blossom. Gravid with loss,
The mazzard, house of mirth, progresses into
Not a house of grief, but of green. Its gross
Weight cleared, to my dole. The dwelling made new

Does not only green, but teem. Blossom lost gives
Rise to gravidity, bestriden by buzzy bumbling
Bees, blues, greys, yellows, whites flutterjives.
Early fructification is humdrum, humbling.

Lankily pediculate pellets pale with leptin
Huddled like sickly swarms from Lowood,
So crimped, so osseous, so taut, so thin,
Thrashed off in throngs, rain-rent, puckered in mud.

Is the frittered fruit affrayed by acid rain?
In April I pace the branch–bridge with pain.

5

In April I pace the branch bridge. With pain
And protracted biding, a sanguine cerise,
Then a vinous violet, then almost an inebriate ebon
Dulcify the spared berylballs to blooded berries.

Less than a tithe of the chartreuse microliths
Are elect to weather, to reach due magnitude.
Though few live to receive the bespoken sapid piths
My gean has gone all out to make it good.

Tonight a tenebrous tryst in and with my gean
Whose susurrus serrulata gives a tenebrae
To bleak bombast of reason and sheen of selfish gene.
Cherries darkly glint. Kissing one glabrous cheek I lie.

I remember scrumping tartars whose cupidity is corpulent.
I recall, with my gean I've made a covenant.

6

I recall, with my gean, my wizened covenant,
Which I arise with cherry-ruddy Aurora
To renew with avid desire to be a tenant
In this Gean, my garden! Will I be worthy, Flora?

Why was I not born and bred within, why did I not learn
To be sportive, responsible, magnanimous, stead-
Fast in, why have I not made myself a dead-sworn
Symbiont with this,my Gean? Why do I still dread

That human kith and kin of mine would wrest me home
Off the body of my Gean, my cottage and companion dear,
House and hearty host, if I refuse to leave home
For fallacious condo? Human, too human, is my fear;

But maugre all I ascend my Gean to glean globed flame
That burns sweet as before capital made it tame.

7

Wild cherry was sweet before capital foisted its frame.
Wild cherry was merry when fruit drafted the treaty:
Succulence charms frugivores to alacrity
To help it live. I'm sorry. I'm sorry. World'll never be the same.

O for when fruit-gathering was a love game!
When humans lost to fructuous trees forty-zero,
When humans were feeble and gardens feral.
Before agroscience staked out its arrogant claims,

Before that springtide scriptorium fell vandalized
By humandroids who chopped to brash alarmed scribes'
Raised assegais and replaced the sundered swords
With plinking printers of gross groaning o's, bloodshot orbs
Who could recognize as cherries? Flowering computerized,
Fructifying forced to print, print, print, the word, word, word.

8

From oneiric print print print, word word word I rise.
Many geans are thus desecrated; o mine is yet fine:
Mutiny against the impulse to homogenize
Has made my Gean uniquely mine!

So I crush my crural flesh against its bark
Marked with many fatiscent mascles
And smudge my milky fingers on its dark
Knubbly elbows, warty calluses and knuckles.

I squirm my flaccid derrière to snail-crawl
Along its thewily trabeated sub-limbs
Towards those bones splayed round super-limbs erectile.
Gawkily I grope, frisk, risk bumbling whims.

I and my Gean copulate by tractable limb-tacks.
My paramazzard I peruse, beloved hapax.

9
My Mazzard is my paramour, beloved only hapax,
(A hapax is a word that lives only once,
Then dies muted in the midden of dead relics.
It flowers on a brief breath, makes only a second's sense.)

I body-write that word, embrace its branches' letters,
Read and rewrite its osmic, somatic brailles
It drybrushes me with cristae of shaggy burrs
Striation of its wood cues the flex of my fibrils.

I and my Gean co-modulate our rhythms of time.
The contours and moves of the hamadryadic sylph
Come with the pulse and pose of her dwelling to rhyme.
She writes herself into this singular hieroglyph.

Girl and Gean are interlocked; the dendrogrammatikos is set.
Cut out one curlicue; our bond falls incomplete.

10

Deleting one dendril its sense will deplete.
But that day is come, that day is come
When the sonnet raves to tell that terrible feat
For our dendrometers are smithereened to detrital strums.

Tartars and their minions in the greenspace meet
When I am truant from, damnedly truant from
My Gean's fecund fork where two wings split
With dentem serrulata to masticate my ashram.

O to ride one more second on its light-leafed wingbeat!
But I come to hearken a twanging alarum
Echoing from the carnage. Decrepit
Ruins posthumous for viaticum.

The garden allée, disencumbered of ranging wings
Of my Gean's bodily imagination, silently dins.

11
My Gean's mangled imagination noiselessly sings.
Know you what comes of this tree-truncating turpitude?
Chasms kerfed and gashed into flesh's gentle twinings.
Much, much more than innocuous chopping of wood.

Are you such spiteful, nauseously mimsy prudes
As to maim this marriage, body and soul, with malisons
So callous? Must you thus pry apart this GeanGirlhood?
Think you it's a righteous untying of lewd liaisons?

Liaisons! And lewd! Is a tree passionately
Cloven to by a vagrant from a species
Long estranged from dendrocracy
Who has wandered back yearning for symbiosis

A maulingstock? Is this Gean a cheap simulacrum
Whose copy can self-replicate ad infinitum?

12
Whose copy can self-replicate ad infinitum
Therefore annulling worth of any one specimen?
Not my Gean. My Gean is not just any specimen
Of what totalitarian taxonomy names *Prunus avium.*

Not this lump of timberum abundiflorum
Nor that field for frolic, playhouse, pleasurable leman,
Not a he, a she, an ita, no singular nomen,
Nor indicator of multiplicity, they, them.

We, ourselves, might say *quod erat demonstrandum*
To what my Gean be, whose every foramen
Conspires with my stoma, my soma, my prana,
Mazzard whose being none is to say, to sum.

If *Prunus avium* lives, my singular Gean having died,
Should I rest complacent, satisfied?

Notes & Acknowledgements

My deep gratitude to Natasha Myers for her epochal recognition of the intrinsic significance of plant-human desmology to our Here and Now: the Planthropocene, and to Michael Marder for teaching me to think phytocentrically.

To the wisdom of aborigines, for the idea of 'songlines,' a map written in songs.

To the University of Arizona Poetry Center, for organizing their vibrantly innovative collaboration between the lore of biodiversity and the insights of art and writing that was called "A Poetic Inventory of Saguaro National Park," on April 16, 2012, for empowering me to imagine this collection as a biosphere and for inspiring me to guide its visitors with a cento piece on which all poems collaborate.

To the many earth-beings that I have rendezvoused, read in books and seen in media, and lived and grown into full flowering in vital intimacy with in my home neighborhood, my university campus, parks, gardens, ruderal spots, and other places and locations near and far, familiar and exotic, virtual or real, for being on this planet and making their worlds so that I may make poems about their poiesis.

To Sir David Attenborough and the vast phalanx of science and nature writers, for their messianic enthusiasm to delight and edify readers with the prismatic mysteries of our living worlds.

To the Black Earth Institute blog for first publishing three poems in this book as part of its Abolitionist/Anticolonial Global Voice feature; the affirmation and encouragement is timely and invaluable for me. These poems are *I Am the Azurrection and the Leaf, Dendrogrammatikos/Treeverse*, and *Commenting with Chlorophytum comosum in the Chthulucene*.

To my kind, dedicated and discerning editors at Atmosphere Press, who first saw this as a worthy miniworld to bring into our world and nurtured its germination and development from raw manuscript to its present proud incarnation.

Finally, to the profound ecological prescience of Emily Dickinson, for connecting me to the spontaneous jouissance of living an ethical existence and making the creative voice of that existence heard. "To be a Flower, is profound/Responsibility—"

About Atmosphere Press

Atmosphere Press is an independent, full-service publisher for excellent books in all genres and for all audiences. Learn more about what we do at atmospherepress.com.

We encourage you to check out some of Atmosphere's latest releases, which are available at Amazon.com and via order from your local bookstore:

Melody in Exile, by S.T. Grant

Covenant, by Kate Carter

Near Scattered Praise Lies Our Substantial Endeavor, by Ron Penoyer

Weightless, Woven Words, by Umar Siddiqui

Journeying: Flying, Family, Foraging, by Nicholas Ranson

Lexicon of the Body, by DM Wallace

Controlling Chaos, by Michael Estabrook

Almost a Memoir, by M.C. Rydel

Throwing the Bones, by Caitlin Jackson

Like Fire and Ice, by Eli

Sway, by Tricia Johnson

A Patient Hunger, by Skip Renker

Lies of an Indispensable Nation: Poems About the American Invasions of Iraq and Afghanistan, by Lilvia Soto

The Carcass Undressed, by Linda Eguiliz

Poems That Wrote Me, by Karissa Whitson

Gnostic Triptych, by Elder Gideon

For the Moment, by Charnjit Gill

Battle Cry, by Jennifer Sara Widelitz

I woke up to words today, by Daniella Deutsch

Never Enough, by William Guest

Second Adolescence, by Joe Rolnicki

About the Author

Lucie Chou is an ecopoet and natural history aficionado. She writes poetry that endeavors to draw from the Romantic tradition to envision the voices and worldings of nonhuman living beings. She has published in the *Entropy* magazine and the *Black Earth Institute Blog*. Residing in mainland China with her beloved houseplants and wildflowers plus their insect and avian paramours, she studies Emily Dickinson, philosophies and artworks about plant-being, contemporary poetry and Richard Powers' eco-novels when not taking walks among feral creatures or drafting poems on foot.